POSITIONAL PLAY

Midfield

by
Allen Wade

Published by
REEDSWAIN INC

Library of Congress Cataloging - in - Publication Data

Wade, Allen
 Positional Play - Midfield

ISBN No. 1-890946-09-5
Copyright © 1997 Allen Wade
Library of Congress Catalog Card Number 97-075738

Reedswain books are available at special discounts for bulk purchase. For details, contact the Special Sales Manager at Reedswain 1-800-331-5191.

Printed in the United States of America.

Credits: Art Direction, Layout, Design and Diagrams • Kimberly N. Bender
Cover Photo: EMPICS

REEDSWAIN VIDEOS AND BOOKS, INC.
612 Pughtown Road • Spring City Pennsylvania 19475
1-800-331-5191 • WWW.REEDSWAIN.COM

Table of Contents

ii

Chapter 1
The Role,
The Responsibilities and
The Attributes of a
Mid-field Player

Success in modern soccer increasingly depends upon the abilities of more and more players to play comfortably and competently in any of the outfield positions. Sophisticated defensive strategies, today, are highly effective in restricting the amount of space available to attackers in all the important areas of the playing pitch and denying space (and therefore time) almost completely in some.

Players who position themselves permanently in specific areas in the hope that, should the ball come, they will conjure up the individual skill to defeat skin-tight markers are unreasonably optimistic. Highly disciplined zonal defensive structures, within which certain defenders mark on a fluid and very tight player-to-player basis are not as easily disturbed as that. Tight markers have to be tempted away from the lines of attack so that quick and late moving support players can enter those areas briefly undetected and unchallenged. These attacking methods require a large number of players to be able to move in and out of different positions at varying speeds, with the perception and the technical skill to be able to loiter long enough, should the ball arrive, to adapt to a different role to optimum effect. This is particularly true when an attacking player enters the penalty area.

A full-back may find himself moving through mid-field positions into wide attacking positions to cross or even to move in on goal and shoot. A central striker may move away from goal, to draw one or more defenders with him, finally filling in for a central back who has seized an opportunity to move into the central space created.

Mid-field players will find themselves often circulating to take up advanced attacking roles or to cover other players moving past them to do so. Modern soccer tactics will become increasingly fluid so that deep defenses face continuously changing problems. The speed and fluidity of change will require them to make judgments and act quicker than stereotyped experience in this position or that will allow.

One of the hallmarks of the successful soccer player today is the extent to which he can set extremely difficult mental and physical problems and give opponents little if any time in which to solve them.

At the very hub of fluid play, involving the continuous interchange of positions, is the mid-field player. As a support player he is closest to the out-and-out attackers and therefore most likely to be able to exchange positions with them. He is also the player most conveniently placed to cover any forward moves by wide or central backs. In fact, of all the players on the field, the mid-field player is best positioned to control and direct the rotational positional interchanges of the kind proposed here.

If coaches are to help young and not so young players to come to terms with the modern game and to realize their ambitions, we have to set out, clearly, the important attributes that the good mid-field player must have at the highest levels of the game. Obviously these attributes will be determined by his role and by his responsibilities in the game and it will make better sense if we examine these first.

1. The role of the mid-field player.
1.1 To link defense to attack.
1.2 To link attack with defense.
1.3 To dominate all mid-field play.
1.4 To control and direct the pace and the directional flow of attacking play.
1.5 To contain, deflect and resist penetration by opposing attackers.
1.6 To press home final attacking play and to shoot to score whenever possible.
1.7 To assume the responsibilities of back defenders should circumstances demand it.

From the above it will be clear that of all the players in the team, the mid-field player is best positioned to direct a team's game plan and the tactical modifications necessary for the game plan's success, hence the title "playmaker" attached to many mid-field players.

Chapter 2
The Responsibilities of The Mid-field Player Arise Logically Out of His Role

2.1 He has a responsibility for presenting the goalkeeper and the backs with passing outlets and interpassing options should they seek to build up controlled counter-attacks through mid-field. To do this he must be prepared to 'show himself' as a pass receiver whatever the difficulties. Alternatively the mid-field player must move to draw opponents away from areas through which players behind and to the side of him may seek to dribble the ball.

2.2 In the event of backs or the goalkeeper seeking to play over mid-field, direct to forward players, mid-field players must move to take up close supporting positions near to or even in front of those forwards.

2.3 In final attacking phases of play, mid-field players must move into the areas from which the most effective passes or shots are likely or as close to those areas as the physiological demands made upon them will allow. For example, a mid-field player committed to defending inside his own penalty area could not be expected to be in the other penalty area following say a quick, three pass move from one end to the other. Even so, he would be expected to be as close to it as circumstances. . . his speed and his state of endurance at that time. . . would permit. The truly great mid-field players DO have the vision, the will and the athletic ability to work inside both penalty areas throughout a full match.

2.4 When ball possession has been lost, mid-field players will play to prevent opponents from playing through the mid-field for the convenience of opposing forward attackers. Generally speaking forward players, when defending, are responsible for containing play among the opposing backs to direct it towards areas pre-determined by the team's defensive game plan. This early containment allows mid-field players to mark opponents tightly enough to increase the likelihood of pass interceptions, incisive tackles or sufficient player-to-player pressure to make further penetration unlikely, even impossible.

2.5 Should opponents penetrate the mid-field defensive line by playing through it or over it, defensive mid-field players must retreat enough to ensure that they are always between the opposing mid-field or back players and goal. To be able to block shots or passes, they must always be 'goal side' of opponents.

2.6 In the event of opponents dribbling the ball past a mid-field defender, he or others must tackle back quickly or take up covering positions behind any defender who has been drawn to confront the attacker with the ball.

From these responsibilities it will be seen that a good mid-field player must be competent in all positions with outstanding skills in some. He is the player who can allow the game to be played frantically and furiously, with no player able to gain time enough to think before acting; on the other hand he is the player who can make time for other players and time, on a soccer pitch, is space. His speed of perception, his technical touch, his willingness to inconvenience himself for the benefit of other players will determine the success or failure of team strategy, of match tactics and of the other players. He in fact determines to a great extent team style which, of course, provides the only sensible basis for player selection, player development and for effective coaching and training in every respect.

Chapter 3
The Principal Attributes of
The Mid-field Player

Putting myself in the position of head scout for a leading professional soccer club, the following are the qualities which I would look for when buying-in replacement mid-field players or when recruiting young players for their first professional contracts.

3.1 The determination and the capability for being directly involved in play for the whole game. This determination goes along with the mid-field player's need to be able to 'read' the game quickly and accurately whatever the circumstances.

3.2 The will to dominate opponents, tactically, technically and athletically, no matter how long it takes. And if he fails in one match against a certain opponent the player will have learned enough to succeed the next time they meet. Outstanding mid-field players are very quick learners: at international level they have to be, they may play against some opponents only once in their playing careers.

3.3 The ability to execute the skills of soccer under sustained and intense pressure which, often, may be very intimidating. The outstanding mid-field player will use his skills with the maximum consideration for his team mates and the minimum consideration for himself. In certain situations, some players benefit from an element of selfishness: when faced with a shooting opportunity for example. In mid-field, selfishness can be a dangerous indulgence.

3.4 The tactical awareness and adaptability to switch from an attacking 'mode' to a defensive 'mode' and back again, repeated many times if necessary, as the flow of even the most frantic game demands. When the going gets tough, mid-field players get going.

3.5 Mid-field players must be able to track and mark opponents competently, thereby improving opportunities for pass interceptions and for early tackles.

3.6 The ability and willingness to rescue team mates in trouble is an important quality. Mid-field players have high degrees of competence at 'fitting in' with their team mates' strengths and weaknesses. Good mid-field players are essentially players' players.

3.7 To bring it all together finally, mid-field players need the all round ability, the perception, the skill. . . and the will. . . to run the whole game the whole time if necessary.

That's asking a lot? Perhaps, but that's why success in the modern game is based upon a team having seven or eight 'mid-field' type players backed up perhaps by two or three 'specialists'. And the specialists will need outstanding attributes in certain circumstances to justify their lack of many of the mid-field player's abilities. Maradonna of Argentina, Beckenbauer of Germany, Gullitt and Van Basten of Holland and other world class players could, at a pinch, play anywhere well.

Goal scoring and the making of scoring opportunities in the most unlikely situations, out of nothing almost, are two obvious circumstances in which it is possible for a limited number of players to have skill so exceptional that they might be excused a lack of other more basic qualities.

Even so, the greater a player's dependency upon limited although outstanding personal skills, the greater the need for another player to balance that player's deficiencies. It follows that to build a team, in which half the players need unusual 'strengths' to compensate for deficiencies among the other half, is a very delicate exercise indeed. When injuries occur or when one or two players lose 'form', replacing the finely integrated parts becomes almost impossible. That was the problem faced in England after winning the World Cup in 1966. It wasn't solved then and has not been solved since.

Chapter 4
Tactical Roles Which a Mid-field Player May Have to Adopt

It is not the purpose of this book to analyze the different strategies and their contributory tactical objectives which prevail in modern soccer. That has been done in my book "Soccer Strategies" which is complementary to this series. Nevertheless team play involves the deployment and use of certain players to fulfill specific and occasionally highly defined tactical roles. The less the degree of rigidity with which players are fitted into these tactical roles, the greater the tactical flexibility which the team is likely to enjoy; the greater the rigidity of tactical deployment, the lesser the team's tactical fluidity.

4.1 The Auxiliary or Floating Striker.

In diagram 1, the players are deployed in an orthodox 1/4-2-4 system. The 'one' represents a goalkeeper, the first 'four' represents the number of back players, the 'two' the number of mid-field players and the final 'four' the number of forwards.

When journalists, television commentators (or coaches and authors like me!) write or speak about team formations or systems, they usually write about 4-2-4, 4-3-3, 4-4-2 and so on. They leave out the goalkeeper and the three figures represent, from left to right, the number of backs, mid-field players and forwards. The numbers are only a rough indication of a team's basic deployment of players; they give no insight into team strategies or into the tactics which a team uses to make the best use of its strengths or to expose opponents' weaknesses.

Systematic team organization, in recent years, has deployed heavy concentrations of players in the back-field area. The tactical thinking being that opponents anxious to exert early pressure against controlled possession play, will have to send large numbers of players forward to do so. In diagrams, 2 and 3 large numbers of players moved forward out of mid-field or out of back defense. This means that a team is exposed to counter attack, not so much on a player-to-player count, where there will always be an extra defender, but because so much more playing space has been liberated. Attackers don't mind man-to-man marking when they have large spaces in which they can maneuver to lose their markers and pull away from close covering defenders.

Nevertheless, many teams still organize for numerical strength in mid-field. Traditionally, the mid-field action area has always been regarded as the key to match control. The mid-field players' defensive roles are closely integrated, with the object

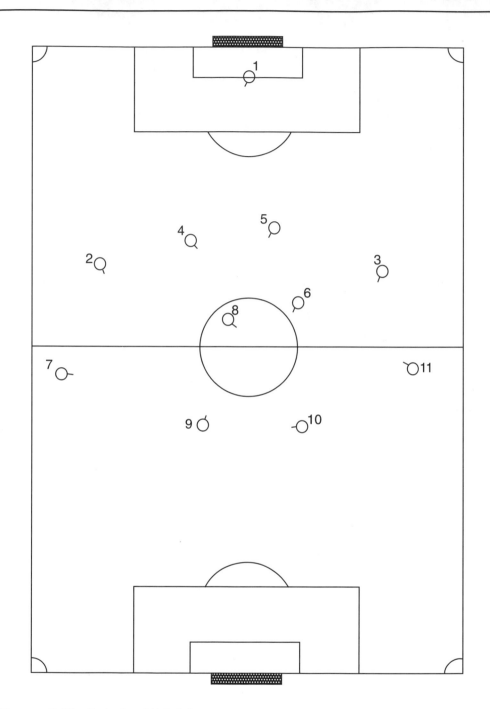

Diagram 1. The Orthodox 1/4-2-4 System.

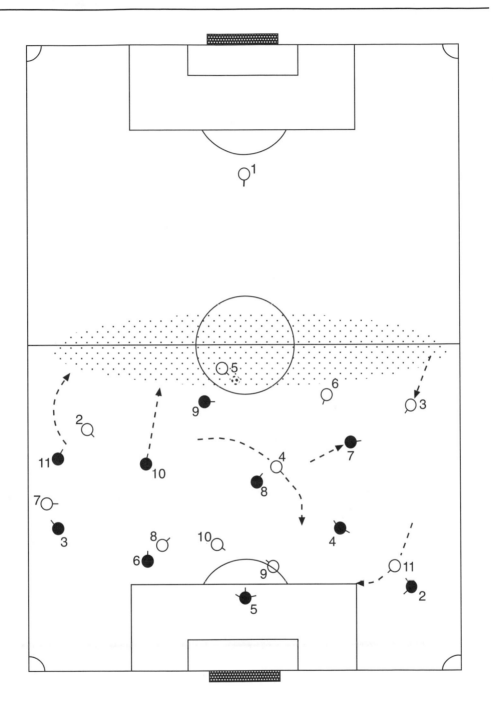

Diagram 2. Exposing space for counter attack by excessive forward movement.

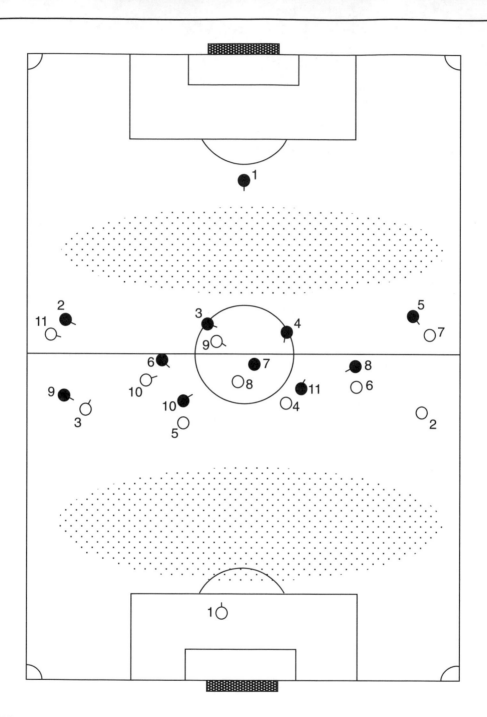

Diagram 3. Concentration of players in midfield allow for counter attacking space.

of producing an impenetrable first defensive curtain, diagram 3.

When teams played to win by scoring as often as possible, even at the expense of conceding goals, opposing mid-field groups usually were equal in numbers. When playing to avoid defeat began to dominate strategical thinking, teams began to organize mid-field deployments so that they outnumbered their opponents, particularly when those opponents had the ball.

Inevitably this led to more and more players being deployed in mid-field, often four from each team, sometimes five. Equally inevitably, the reinforcement of mid-field was achieved at the expense of forward attacking strength. This meant that to attack effectively, one or more mid-field players had to become auxiliary strikers whenever a counter strike was a reasonable possibility. In diagram 4, as black 8 sees a teammate likely to gain possession of the ball, he drifts wide of the immediate area of action and appears disinterested in what is going on. His aim is to move quickly and unnoticed into the shaded area whenever there is a reasonable possibility of a pass from one of the other mid-field players directly up to one of the strikers. Both strikers are tightly marked and covered, in this example, by a free centre back or sweeper, white 5. Without someone to whom they can 'lay off' passes to build up penetrating moves, counter attack will flicker briefly and die. Black 8, acting as an auxiliary striker, gives the real strikers options from which the counter attack can develop further.

In diagram 5, where the mid-field battle is being fought in an area to one side of the pitch between eight players, one player who is likely to be successful in entering the shaded area undetected is black 7. His approach must be indirect. A direct run will attract the attention of his marker, white 6. An indirect approach is less likely to draw an opponent into following and if black 7 's move is deceptive enough, he may even get into the target area unnoticed by any opposing mid-field players. His movement forward may be picked up by one or more of the three central backs. . . if they are awake! That is why he must show no sign of making his 'sneak' run until a pass to the orthodox strikers is on its way. Strikers black 9 and 10 will try to draw their markers apart before a pass is 'on' so that the space available for the auxiliary striker will be difficult to counter unless the sweeper is drawn forward.

This is exactly what the attackers want to happen, diagram 6. The back defense is drawn 'square' and highly vulnerable to through passes.

Mid-field players who have excellent technical skills may set up apparently indirect, even negative, inter-passing moves. They do so primarily to attract the attention of as many opponents as possible and draw them towards the ball. This may allow a mid-field player or any other player for that matter to drift out of the action to attack the space in front of the strikers.

These qualitative considerations are crucially important to a team developing subtle penetrating skills. They are considerations conveniently ignored by coach statisticians who want the game played predictably, by numbers almost, to whom quality has no importance because statisticians can't measure it.

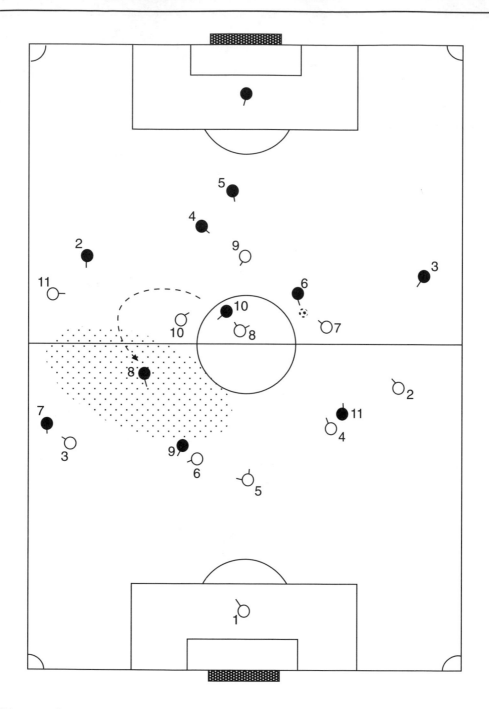

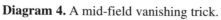

Diagram 4. A mid-field vanishing trick.

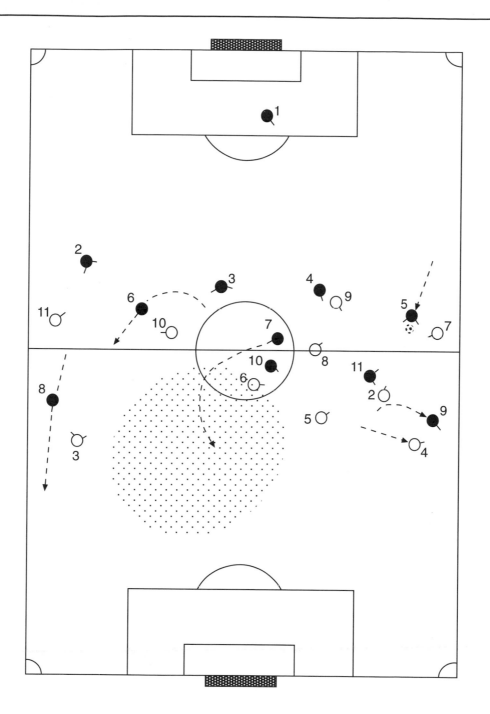

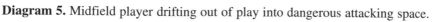

Diagram 5. Midfield player drifting out of play into dangerous attacking space.

Beware of coach statisticians bearing soccer facts!

In diagram 6, where the teams are using variations of the 1/4-2-4 system, the player who intends to become an auxiliary central striker is black 11. His two mid-field playmakers, black 6 and 8, will look for the opportunity to play high quality passes into the feet of the two central strikers or to the deep wide attacker, black 7. As soon as black 11 sees the probability of a pass being delivered into the central space, he will set off across field to attack it. It will take a quick thinking and an even quicker moving full-back to react to his run in time. In recent years it has been tactically fashionable for defending teams to station one player in the space in front of the central defenders. This 'picket' player, black 6 in diagram 7, patrols the shaded area and makes it much more difficult for passes to be played into the feet of the central strikers. If the defending team plays with a free back, the picket player can drop back into that role should the free back be drawn into wide covering or challenging positions, Diagram 8. We shall consider this defensive mid-field role in detail later in this chapter.

The picket player is ideally positioned to watch for mid-field players attempting to steal into central space. In these circumstances it will pay an attacking team to move a mid-field player into the space marked by the picket player. There will be no weakening of either team in the mid-field struggle since both teams have taken one player out of it. At least the remainder will have that much more space in which to play!

In his new position, 'reverse marking' his defensive opponent almost, the auxiliary striker's main aim, always, will be to threaten the space on the far side of the picket player. Diagram 9. As attacking play moves from side to side, the piquet player will adjust his position with it. But the 'pulling' effect of the extra striker behind him makes this a dangerous risk. Any defender allowing an opponent to gain a blind-side position so near to goal is taking his life in his hands. Normally in these circumstances the picket player will drop back and wider to mark his opponent. Diagram 9. This enables the auxiliary attacker to control the movements of a defender whose role and effectiveness depend to a great extent on his freedom from specific marking duties.

If another mid-field player can drift out of the mid-field struggle and reappear to move quickly and late into the space to the side of the picket player and in front of the regular strikers, the opportunities for penetrating the opponents' last defensive line will be opened up once again.

In attack, there is one certain way of affecting the disposition of opposing defenders and that is by sending attackers in to 'collect' them. If the attackers always 'pull' in the opposite direction to the flow of play, they will set their opponents very difficult marking and even more difficult covering problems.

Some teams position a floating striker permanently in the space in front of the two central strikers but any tactical move executed on a permanent basis destroys the effect of surprise. Permanent tactical deployments in attack are self defeating other than where opposing teams are incapable of 'reading' play of course.

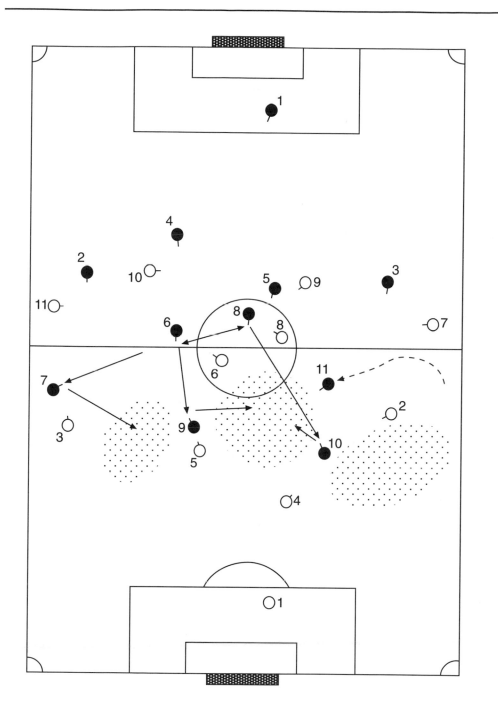

Diagram 6. Unexpected moves by attackers into key spaces.

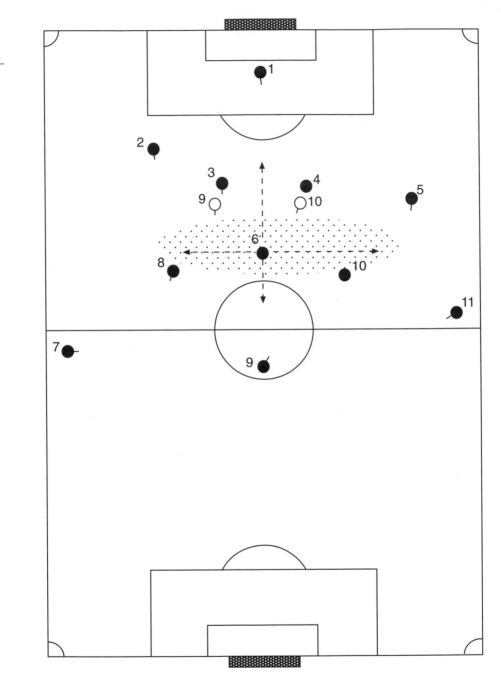

Diagram 7. A picket player's main area of responsibility.

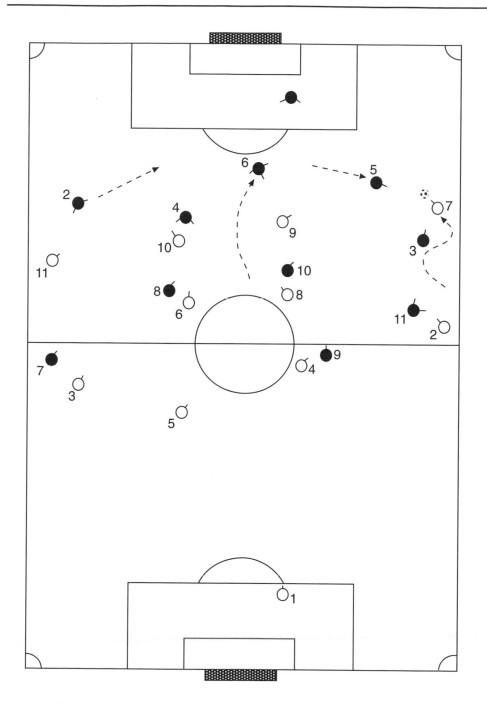

Diagram 8. The picket player, black 6, assumes the free back role.

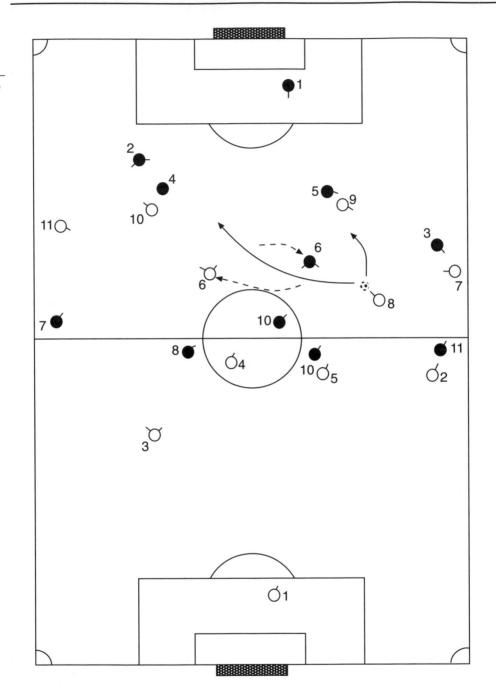

Diagram 9. White attacker 6 tries to pull the picket player, black 6, out of position by moving onto his blind-side.

The Dutch team of the early seventies was so fluid and involved so many players in its attacking build-ups and strikes on goal that opponents were hard pressed to know who to mark and to what extent they dared continue the marking. Diagram 10. The almost continuous circulation of seven or eight players, sometimes slowly, sometimes exploding into fierce attacking runs to head or shoot for goal, meant that defenders were always in danger of being drawn away from or to the extreme fringe of the areas in which danger was likely to occur. The sophistication of tightly integrated zonal defense, for ultimate effectiveness, depends upon defenders' skill and confidence in transferring tight marking responsibilities on potential strikers from defender to defender, smoothly and easily. When the number of attackers to be picked up, marked and then transferred is six, seven or eight, the understanding and confidence between defenders has to be almost telepathic. It rarely is!

4.2 Mid-field Sweeper.

Many teams face the painful problem of what to do with the supremely skillful, very influential but aging mid-field player who begins to lose whatever speed he had and some of the stamina. If he is allowed to try to control play as he always did, inevitably he will cause the game to be played to suit himself and in such a way as to enable him to hide his deficiencies. More and more passes will be played to feet . . . especially to his feet; more and more running will be required of the players around him, to compensate for the running which he cannot or chooses not to do. Certain players will be required to carry out his tackles and his marking assignments; if they are not, the team may be seriously unbalanced in defense.

In the 1978 World Cup in Argentina, Spain had just such a player in Juan Asensi, the F. C. Barcelona mid-field orchestrator. It seemed that every pass, almost, was drawn to or dispatched from his educated feet. He was beautiful to watch but the overall profitability of Asensi's total domination of his team's mid-field play was modest. In the same tournament and in keeping with their long tradition of classical mid-field controllers, Austria's play-maker, Herbert Prohaska, was absolutely in the Asensi mold, with much the same result. Controlling the flow and tempo of the game, with total precision and considerable artistry, without producing the conclusive cutting edge, incisive goal-making passes, is self indulgence. And yet an aging player's tactical know-how is invaluable.

Some teams have solved the problem by pulling such a player back behind the basic mid-field unit of players. Diagram 11. From this position, the playmaker can see and direct the defensive activity of the players immediately in front of him. He himself has only the occasional need to run to tackle or to intercept. Both are so much easier for him because he has more time to 'read' situations leading to through passes and to intercept them. When he has the ball, a positive run of five to ten yards, if he feels like it, is likely to free other mid-field players to receive passes behind their opponents. All they need to do is to move into blind-side positions against their nearest opponents, diagram 12, thus making space for the playmaker's run and themselves available for positive passes.

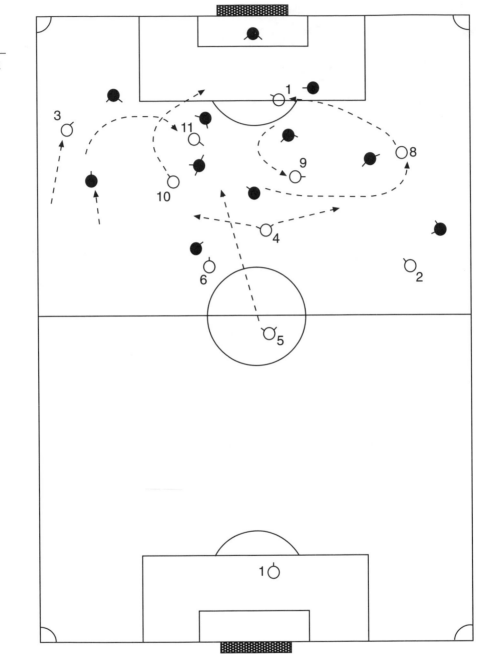

Diagram 10. Fluent rotational interchange of position.

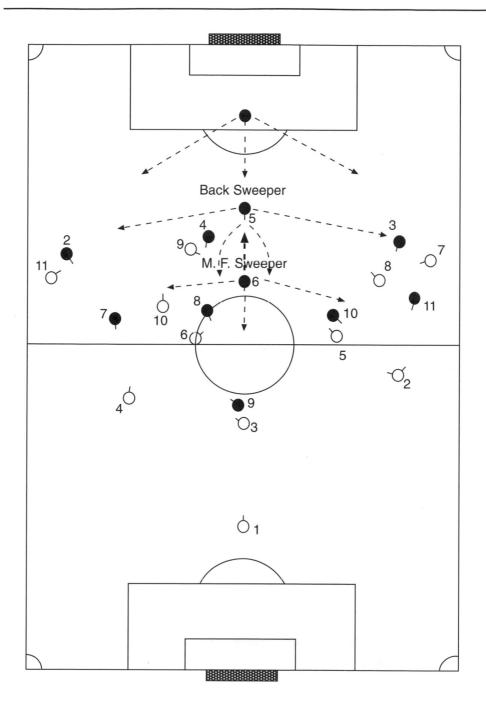

Diagram 11. The mid-fielder sweeper controlling mid-field in defense and attack.

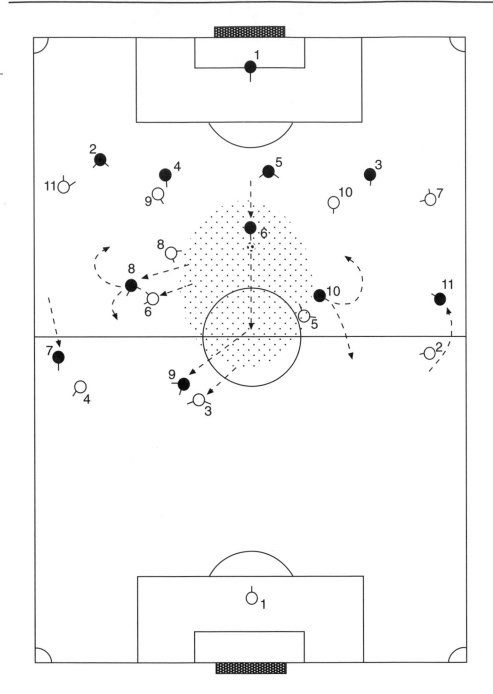

Diagram 12. Black attackers 'showing' blind side positions for black 6 with the ball.

Should any of the orthodox mid-field players gain possession under intense opposing pressure, there is always an escape outlet close by, usually behind them, the veteran controller. In this mid-field sweeper role, the player is acting as a link between mid-field and the backs in much the same way as the orthodox libero or free back fills a similar role between the backs and the goalkeeper. The essential difference is that the mid-field sweeper's role is much more positive. His primary purpose is to support and direct attacking moves: filling key spaces or marking dangerous opponents is very much a secondary consideration. Remember, the mid-field prompter, as he might be more accurately described is likely to have definite limitations, hence his deployment in that role. The free back or libero should have none.

The prompter will have license to move into any position across the whole attacking front in order to offer himself for passes to keep up the momentum of attacking play. Mid-field players in front of him, particularly the wide ones, are able to move forward aggressively into counter attacking positions knowing that whatever their aging team mate cannot do, he can still release accurate and perfectly weighted through passes.

The late Helmut Schoen, the German Bundes Coach and the most successful international coach of modern times, suffered from an embarrassment of riches in mid-field. He had two master playmakers at his disposal, Franz Beckenbauer and Gunther Netzer, together with a highly respected mid-field player's player, the vastly tried and trusted Wolfgang Overath. Ulli Hoehness had already made his name in the 1972 European Championship team while the up and coming Rainer Bonhof threatened all the established players' positions. Beckenbauer became the libero in every respect. Netzer, a mid-field player of extraordinary vision and passing skill, had little appetite for the 'chores' of the game, the grit and graft of tackling, covering, chasing and pressuring. He saw himself as the orchestra conductor sharing the baton occasionally with Beckenbauer, diagram 13. Unfortunately, to win matches in the cauldron which is World Cup competition, two players only occasionally committed to industrious action is too few. Tragically for those of us. . . including Helmut Schoen himself. . . to whom outstanding soccer was a matter for artistry rather than industry, Netzer's deficiencies outweighed his talents and he had to go. The German press and the public demanded a German victory.

Looking back, it might have been worth Coach Schoen's while to ask Beckenbauer to resume the mid-field role in which he became a world class player at nineteen years of age, while allowing Netzer to drop back into the sweeper position. Be that as it may, successful or not, it was a sheer joy to watch them playing together.

When Netzer was playing successfully and positively in the German national team, leading up to the European Championship team of 1972, the two other mid-field players, Ulli Hoehness and Herbert Wimmer, were responsible for making all the forward runs whenever Netzer got the ball. . . which was often! Their forward runs, diagram 13, had to be made for two very good reasons; first, to achieve the auxiliary striker positions already referred to; second, to draw opponents away from the area in which Netzer needed to 'work' the ball in order to deliver the elegant and

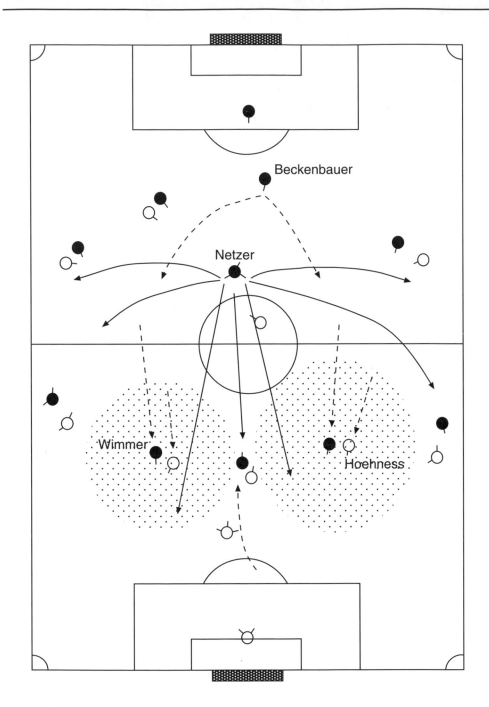

Diagram 13. Germany '72.

deadly accurate forward passes for which he was famous. To be effective, Hoehness and Wimmer had to be perpetual motion players. They had to move to support their tightly marked forward pass receivers and if the passes broke down they had to get back even quicker because whatever Netzer could do, defend he could not. . . or would not. . . which comes to the same thing.

In his later years, in my view, Gunther Netzer became more concerned with the elegance of his delivery than with its effectiveness. Passes were sprayed all over the field but less and less for the convenience of the strikers and their hard working support players and more and more because the passes looked good. In these circumstances, there comes a time when even the most willing of runners begin to ask if their journeys are really necessary and, as they get older, they simply refuse to make them.

4.3 Wide Attacker.

The concentration of large numbers of players in mid-field was achieved, initially, by withdrawing one or both wide attackers. The tactical objectives of some teams were:
  (a) to produce a double curtain in defense covering the whole pitch whereby the distance between any two defenders rarely exceeded fifteen yards and was usually less.
  (b) to tempt the opposing full-backs as far away from goal, and their central defenders as possible and
  (c) to develop close overlapping links in defense and attack between the wide backs and the players in front of them, diagram 14.

The 1958 Brazilian World Cup team, the team regarded by some as one of the best three national teams of all time, is regarded as the initiator of the 4-2-4 system. In fact, when defending. . . which admittedly wasn't often. . . Mario Zagallo, recently the highly successful Brazil national coach, then an orthodox, stick-to-the-line winger, dropped deep into the left mid-field position. The team's defensive deployment was always a goalkeeper, a free back, three marking backs, three mid-field defenders and three attackers, diagram 15.

Zagallo became a modern, highly competent all rounder. He had the skills, the vision and the intelligence to fill in for attackers, midfielders or backs as circumstances demanded.

Gradually orthodox, out and out wingers disappeared to be replaced by mid-field players who developed some of the skills. . . or none. . . of the old fashioned winger. However, as some sort of sense began to prevail, coaches saw that without forward flank attackers, they couldn't expect to draw defenders away from goal. The part wingers, part mid-field players had to practice to develop the special skills needed by wide attackers: the ability to dribble past full-backs on the outside to deliver crosses from as near to the goal line as possible: the ability to fake an outside dribble and to cut inside a wide back for a shot on goal: the vision to exploit opportunities for instant long, cross-field passes to the strikers. These passes had to be seen

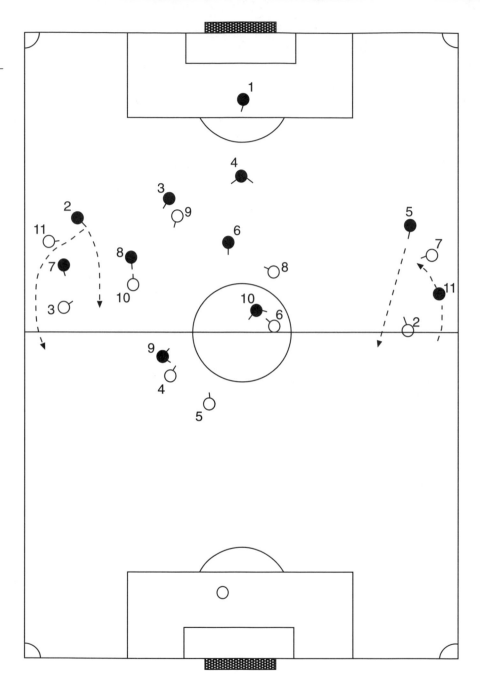

Diagram 14. Overlapping interchanges between wide backs and wide attackers.

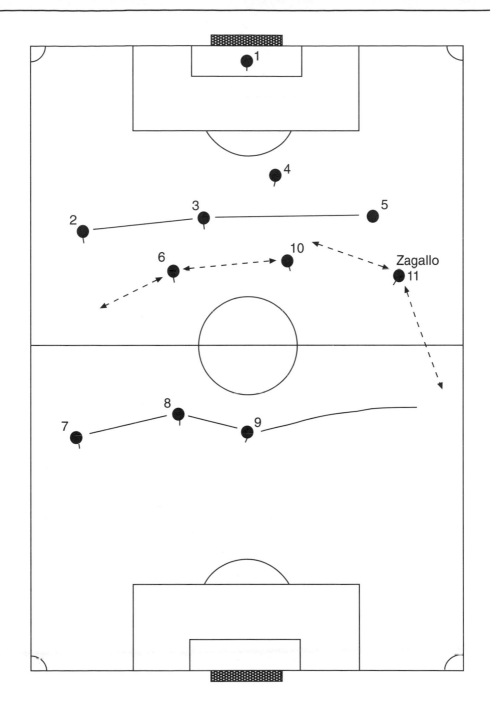

Diagram 15. Brazil '58' 4:2:4 changing to 4:3:3 in defense.

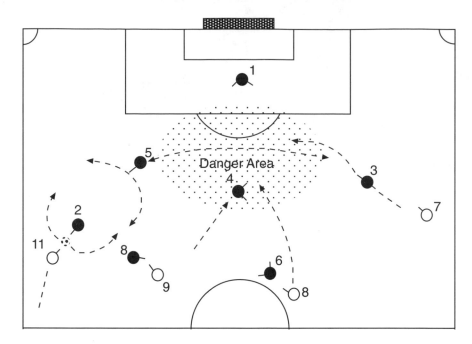

Diagram 16. The sweeper over drawn to the flanks. The need for his 'far-side' back or the picket player to fill in for him.

and delivered instantly since the strikers found it increasingly difficult to achieve reasonable striking positions against ever tighter marking with, in most countries, a free central back covering the markers and the space behind them. Some countries committed their full-backs into man-to-man duels against the opposing wide attackers and where this happened, there arose additional justification for the deployment of a mid-field player in the picket position already referred to. When the sweeper was drawn out wide to cover the space behind the advanced full-backs, the piquet player offered immediate security. Diagram 16.

Other countries settled for the attrition which arose out of two teams withdrawing eight or nine. . . occasionally ten. . . players into zonal defensive structures behind the ball as soon as possession was lost. . . or looked like being lost. . . or sooner! Where this occurred, the wide mid-field player found it extremely difficult to achieve the highly desirable goal line crossing position. Two defenders usually covered by a third meant that two attackers, the wide mid-fielder and his supporting full-back, assuming that he was supporting, being outnumbered had little chance.

Forward looking countries developed players skillful enough to refuse to bow to the extra defender. By supporting flank attacking moves with numbers these countries brought about a renaissance in wide attacking play which is, of course, fundamental to any tactics devised to open up central defense.

To attack successfully through the centre, the build up must be on the flanks and to attack successfully round the flanks, it is important to build up the initial attack

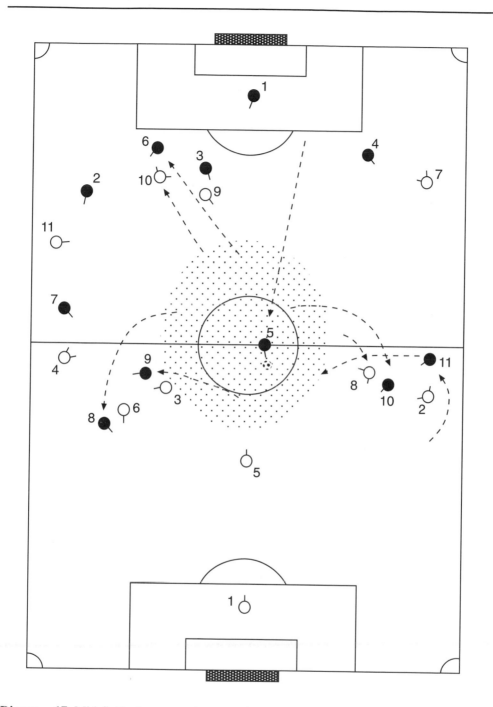

Diagram 17. Mid-field players moving out of mid-field to tempt markers with them in order to open up mid-field for attacking developments.

threat centrally. Diagram 17.

Any threat of penetration in wide positions will tend to draw defenders away from the centre, leaving central defense that much more vulnerable to sudden switches in play. Any threat of penetration centrally will draw the wide defenders into the centre.

Reference has been made to the commitment of significant numbers of defenders to player-to-player duels in which, wherever an attacker went, his marker would follow. Tightly marked players must be free to choose where to go to try to shake off their markers. . . or to take their markers into areas wherein neither player can contribute to play! Against unshakable marking, it may be necessary for teams to play most of a game without one or even more players from each team. Alternatively, the marked players will move away from their normal positions, taking their markers with them, to open up the space into or through which other players may move. The timing and the integration of moves between backs and mid-field payers or between mid-field players and forwards and even between backs and forwards is the secret. . . if there is a secret. . . to attacking developments in the future.

The more that teams base their play on functional stereotypes. . . powerful wide backs who kick the ball. . . and sometimes opponents. . . out of sight; lighthouses as central backs, tall enough to see danger over the horizon and too tall to see it beneath their feet; mid-field players so busy working to deny time and space to opponents that they never have any themselves; strikers who are better equipped for the track than for the soccer field and so on, the greater their problems in adapting to modern soccer.

You don't agree? Take a look at the international records of some of the so-called advanced soccer nations in the world.

4.4 The Picket Player or Anchor Man.

We have already seen how attacking tactics have tried to exploit the space between and in front of the central backs in such ways as to make cover and interception by the libero very difficult. We have also examined the role of the mid-field sweeper in offering passing outlets to all defending players from a position between mid-field and back-field. The use of a picket player to hold a position in the area in front of the central backs has been the logical outcome. He is more a part of a defensive structure than an attacker, nevertheless his holding position makes him available to all back players as a passing safety valve. In a similar way to the 'libero', the back sweeper if you like, the picket player can assist back (and mid-field) players to establish comfortable, unhurried possession of the ball, the first requirement for accurate counter-attack.

Additionally, the picket player blocks any opponent attempting to attack the space between the central backs. Before this tactical development, any opposing mid-fielder prepared to run the ball directly at the heart of the opposing defense posed difficult problems for a libero. Should he move forward in front of the back markers to meet the attacking threat? If so, when? When moving forward should he do so quickly and as late as possible or more cautiously and earlier?

Should he move all the way to close down his oncoming opponent fully or should his aim be to make the opponent pass the ball?

All defenders dislike problems: defenders with full covering responsibilities most of all. A picket player ensures that covering problems are minimized.

In some countries, the sweeper (free back or libero) is required to provide cover across the whole back line behind any defender. Covering close to one of the wide backs, he must leave central and dangerous shooting positions exposed. The defense can easily be unbalanced unless the 'far side' back is particularly perceptive in moving into covering positions. Diagram 18. Even so, should attacking play be suddenly switched back to the centre or beyond it a sweeper may not be able to regain his central covering and intercepting position in time. The 'far side' covering fullback is caught between two attackers, the central one he must mark tightly, leaving the player beyond free and dangerous.

If the sweeper is committed to a very wide position, a picket player can drop back as a temporary central sweeper. If the attack moves back towards the centre, the picket player only vacates his temporary role when the regular sweeper has regained his central position. Diagram 19.

The essential feature of the picket player's play is his ability to judge when to move forward and 'onto' an opposing attacker and when not. We have already seen how opponents may send in a player to 'reverse mark' a picket player and try to pull him away from his main area of operation.

This causes a kind of 'elastic band' effect. The further the picket player moves in one direction, the greater the degree of 'pull' exerted by his opponent in the opposite direction.

An effective picket player must know to the yard the distance which he can concede to an opponent, on his blind-side, while being sure that, should play be switched across towards that opponent, he (the picket player) can move across to block the danger. This is precisely the same judgment of speed and distance required by the sweeper. Of course both players have some degree of cover when permitting some threat on their blind-sides. In the twin central back system favored. . . dangerously and mistakenly. . . by English teams, one-versus-one situations, in which an attacker is allowed to position himself on his marker's blind-side, are easily achieved. If English central backs were more noted for their speed than for their size, this might be understandable.

The Argentine World Cup (1978) winning team included a number of players who achieved world wide renown. Ardiles who became an outstanding success in English soccer: Villa, not quite so successful but a player with more talent than perhaps he realized: Passarella who enjoyed a memorable career in Italy while Kempes performed with great distinction for Valencia in Spain. In my opinion, by far the most important player, little known outside Argentina and not highly rated inside it, was Americo Gallego, a picket player to perfection.

Argentina's wide backs were no more than ordinary defenders, better with the ball

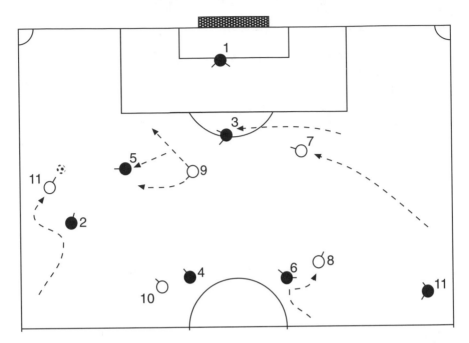

Diagram 18. The far-side back filling central space but caught between two attackers.

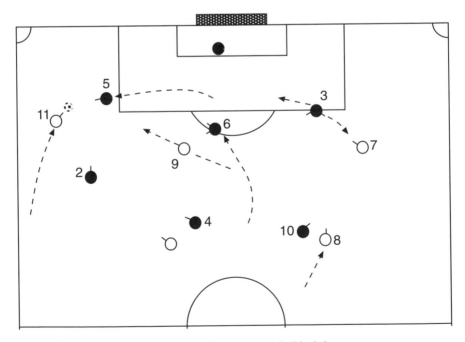

Diagram 19. The picket player, black 6, sweeps up behind the sweeper.

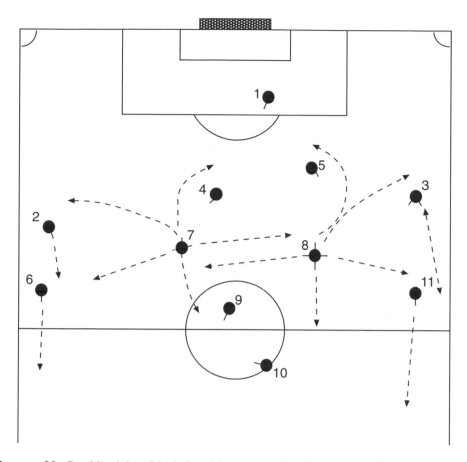

Diagram 20. Double picket, Black 7 and 8, protect all the backs and offer midfield support.

than getting it. This meant that Passarella, the sweeper, had to use his considerable speed and often last ditch tackling skill to cover the flanks. This meant that someone had to have the deep sense of responsibility to act as second sweeper, to watch for any threat against central space and be skillful enough to deflect it away from goal and into the hands. . . or rather the feet. . . of the mid-field defenders. Gallego did this admirably and he was also capable of offering the surest support to the considerable talents of mid-field controller Osvaldo Ardiles.

Since that time, we have seen some countries deploy two players in the picket player role, diagram 20. This has been part of a general trend towards heavy deployment of players in the back field areas. This has allowed for optimum security in defense and guaranteed control of ball possession when it is regained. The idea being that if a team has six players (five and a sweeper) at the back, it is unlikely that opponents will send five or six players forward to contest possession although a good question may be, "Why not?" In a European Cup Final within recent years one of the participants had six backs plus the sweeper behind, two

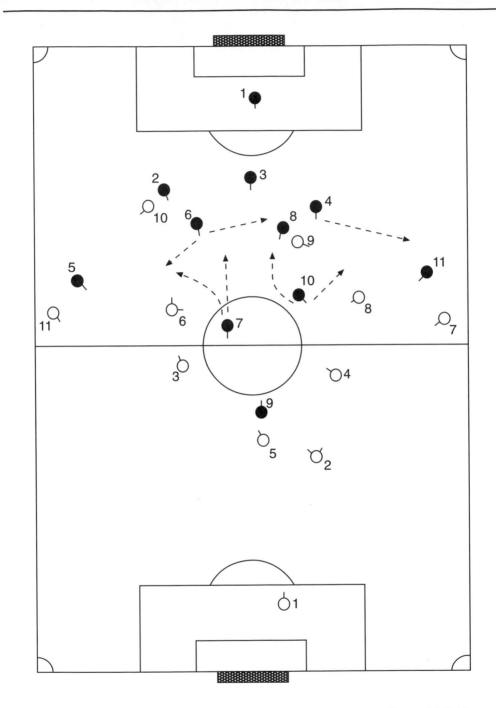

Diagram 21. Six backs and a sweeper 30 plus two picket players, auxiliary mid-field defenders.

players in mid-field. . . to all intents and purposes picket players. . . leaving only one player forward, diagram 21.

Not the most optimistic of strategical deployments! Nonetheless, in a match which required the highest concentration (in case the only exciting move in twenty minutes of play happened to be missed!) this negative strategy of giving nothing away enabled the team using it to win on a penalty shoot-out. The tactical use of a picket player to do nothing other than to deny opponent's space is unnecessary and offends against simple principles of play.

Triangulation has always been the basis for sensible team play in defense and in attack. In diagram 22, we can see how different mid-field units are deployed using triangular principles to ensure all round support and therefore progress and penetration in attack. Similar deployments give cover and double cover if necessary when a team is defending. Diagram 23.

Players must be brought up, from the very earliest days of their commitment to the game, to see it as two complementary problems. The first asks each player to find out what he and his team must do to score goals most effectively. The second asks each player and the team (in that order) to find out how to take the ball away from opponents while preventing them from scoring.

Learning how to answer those questions requires clear thinking and very good coaching and yet the answers are extremely simple as this book, I hope, shows.

4.5 The First Curtain in Defense.

Reference has been made to the use by many teams of defensive curtains; one, two or even, in extreme circumstances, three. The idea of defensive curtains came first from Italy where, at the time, defense was regarded as a matter of filling the key attacking areas with defenders and using high concentrations of defenders to entice opponents into taking risks beyond their capabilities; thereby losing the ball. . . or giving it away. The 'drawing' of the curtain depended upon a controlled, 'funneledí'retreat by seven, eight or nine players into a highly concentrated defensive structure in front of the penalty area. Diagram 24.

The rearmost curtain, comprising the sweeper and the three or four backs gave ground while marking forward attackers very tightly. The front curtain of four players encouraged opponents to keep the ball while drawing them into impossibly tight areas, thereby increasing the probability of interceptions or tackles.

The strategical priority was the withdrawal of all the players in both curtains before any active attempts to regain the ball were promoted. If opponents gave the ball away, that was a different matter. . . and faced with Italian 'encouragement', British teams often did. The great temptation for attackers playing against defenders retreating. . . running away, as it were. . . is to speed up play beyond the experience and the skills of the players. This, almost inevitably, means that the ball is given away.

For young players and for the coaches handling their development, it is a 'must' for players to be encouraged, even required, to become comfortable in using their skills

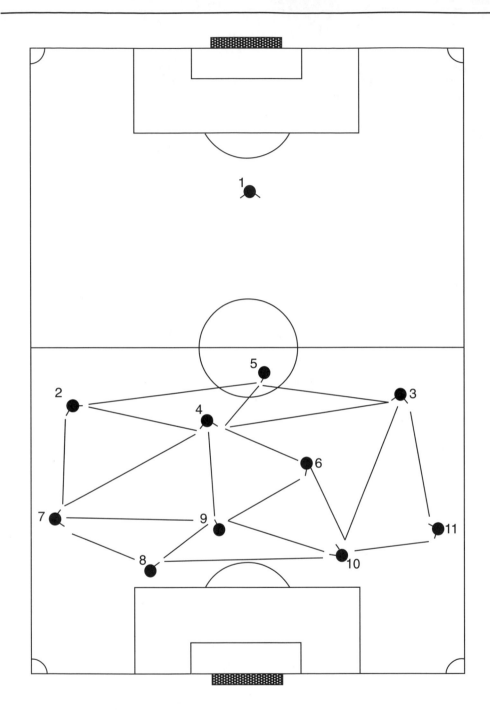

Diagram 22. Mid-field tight triangulation linking up with attackers.

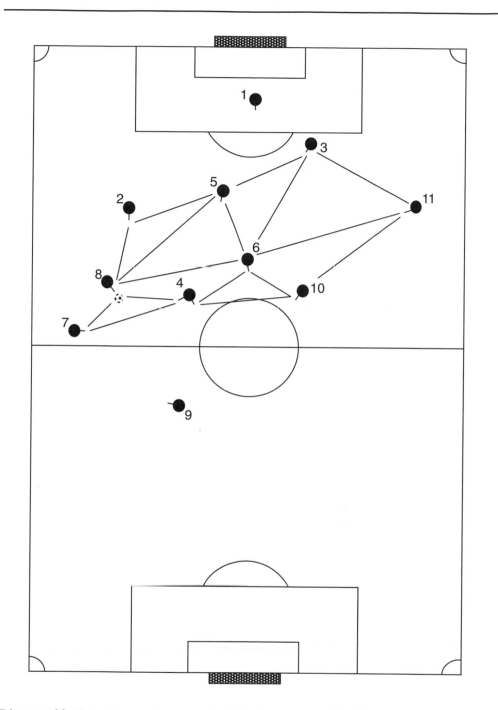

Diagram 23. Tight triangulation near the ball gives cover and double cover in defense.

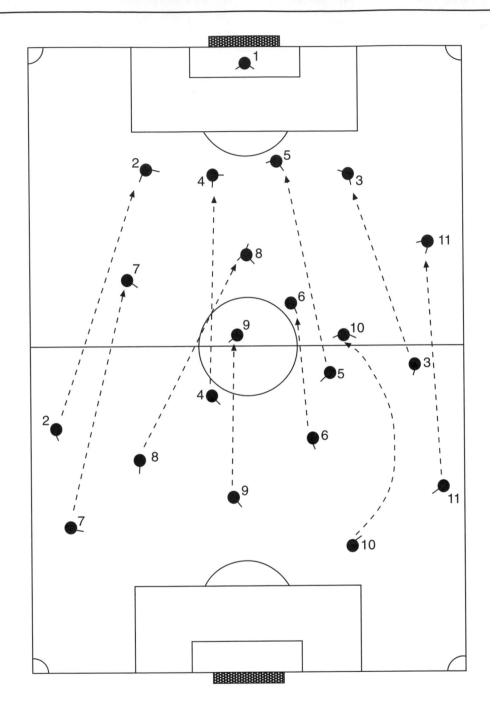

Diagram 24. Funnelling and retreating in defense.

at acceptable speeds before progressing to levels of play at which they have to play at a faster pace. Any idea that the sooner they are exposed to speed and pressure the better, must be resisted at all costs. The most harmful influence in the game today is increasingly earlier exposure to highly competitive leagues and the insatiable demand for success in them. Unremitting competitive pressure is harmful enough to experienced professionals let alone to six, seven and eight year olds. For the vast majority of young players, whose skills are still fragile, the pin-ball soccer induced by excessive competition destroys skill and initiative.

Full retreating and funneling defense is difficult to penetrate other than by sending players into forward positions to equal opposing defenders numerically and thereby to control them. The first curtain, produced by mid-field players withdraws to a pre-arranged distance from goal, outside shooting range. The players forming the curtain allow any player with the ball to penetrate slightly. Diagram 25. The nearest defenders close in and increase the pressure all round him. (i.e. players are concentrated in a tighter area from which they step up activity aimed at taking the ball away from the attacker or causing him to give it away.) The enclosure cuts off his passing outlets and makes him depend exclusively on his own ball holding and dribbling skills. Fewer and fewer players have them at a high enough level. And there's a tip for soccer teachers and coaches undecided how to spend their time to greatest advantage!

The attractiveness of curtain defense, or *catenacchio* as it was called in Italy, lay in collective responsibility. Players. . . especially high class players. . will deny personal responsibility for defensive errors at almost any cost. Curtain defense allowed individuals to 'hide' within its folds which was a strength but, when taken to extremes, a weakness. A player lacking defensive commitment would arrive to make (fake) a tackle a milli-second after the opponent made his move. The same player, seeing an opponent making a run which was obviously a fake, ran to cover the run, which meant he got out of the responsibility for gritting his teeth to stop more dangerous opponents. These 'invisible men' of defensive play were always in covering positions at rear headquarters, rarely if ever in the front line trenches where the real action was taking place.

In these escape routes for players with poor defensive commitments lay the ultimate failure of the system. Too many players didn't want to graft and struggle; too many did want to float about on the fringe of the real action waiting to pick up the mistakes caused by the hard working minority.

In any defensive strategy, the system devised will be only as strong as the extent to which each and every player understands and applies the principles of defense consistently.

Gradually as the weaknesses of dependence upon the curtain 'system' became apparent, coaches used it as the basis for pressure points moving out and onto any player with the ball. One defender in the front curtain became a 'nose' defender, a description which will be clearly understood by followers of American Football. Diagram 26 (a).

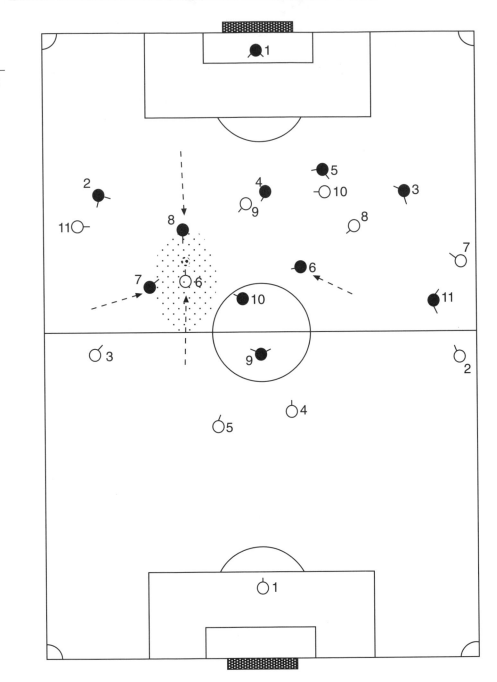

Diagram 25. Entrapment of the ball runner, white 6, in *catencchio* or curtain defense.

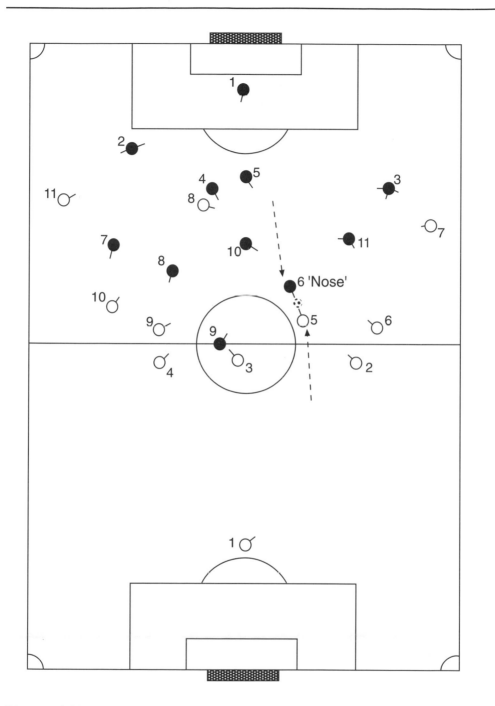

Diagram 26 (a). Using a 'curtain' defense to pressure opposing attackers into losing possession: the deployment of 'nose' defenders.

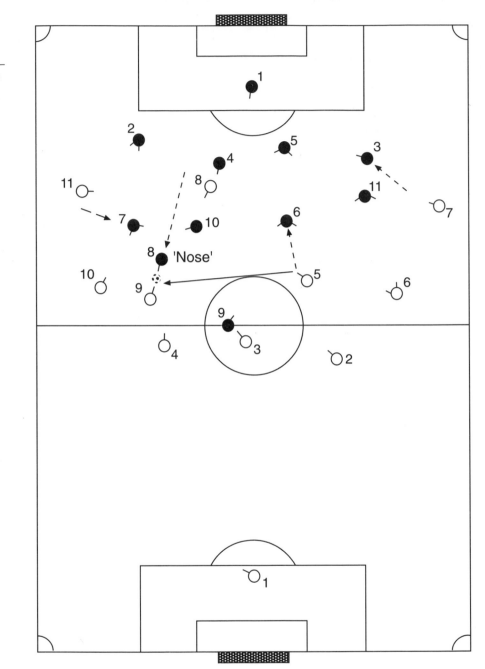

Diagram 26 (b). 'Nose' defense where attacking thrust having switched to white 9, black 8 moves out to become the nose (the first) defender.

As play was deflected across the field, one player in the front curtain acting as the nose defender would drop back to be replaced by another. Diagram 26 (b).

In addition to the application of more positive pressure by the front curtain of defenders, certain back players, usually the one or more central backs were made to mark the advanced attackers 'touch tight' whenever those attackers occupied or moved within the key shooting area. Diagram 27.

Controlling a game is best achieved when players know, within reason, what each is trying to do.

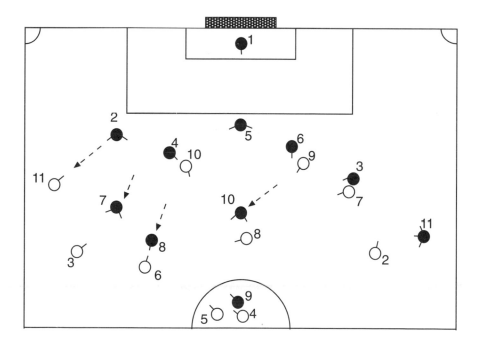

Diagram 27. Man-to-man, touch tight marking by players in the back curtain of defense. Black 8 is the 'nose' defender in this black 8 is the nose defender here.

Chapter 5
Individual and Group Tactical Skills

Tactics are moves which are made, or which players pretend to make, to enable them to use their technical and athletic skills decisively. Tactics are the means by which players, individually or with other players, set problems for opponents; their purpose is to disrupt and confuse opponents and to dislocate their normal patterns of play. Tactics can be physical or psychological; usually they are both.

From the description of the general role and the responsibilities of a mid-field player, it is obvious that the all round demands on him mean that he should aim to be master of all aspects of play. And by implication, he should have all the basic skills required of any player, defender or attacker, at very high levels. These skills, together with outstanding athletic capabilities will enable him to exert match winning control for the whole of ninety minutes.

In the final analysis, however skillful a player is, he will only dominate and defeat opponents if, when necessary, he gets to the ball first.

The younger the player, the more his individual skill makes him a winner. As he grows older he will need the help of other players to defeat opponents. Eventually all players need not only skill, they need the physiological capacity, the engine if you like, and the mental sharpness to see them through. If any one of these three qualities is missing, the player will struggle.

There is a mistaken belief that skill and know-how allows veteran players to get by. Not when he meets opponents who know how to expose his deficiencies it won't. Players running at and past him with the ball will leave him for dead. . . but more of that later.

5.1 Deception.

To succeed in the highest class, in the World Cup Final for example, a mid-field player must be cunning. He must have the ability to hide his real intentions whatever he happens to be doing. . . especially when he appears to be doing nothing!

When about to trap the ball, he must be able to change his move into a pass.

When moving to trap the ball left, he should be able to change to the right and with no give-away signs.

When jumping to head the ball, he should be able to change his header into, say, a chest controlling movement.

Signaling his intention to give a simple ten yard pass, with no change in his kicking action other than in acceleration, he must be able to lengthen and lift his pass from ten to forty yards.

Set to deliver an obvious pass, he needs the option of being able to explode instantly into a powerful, dribbling run.

All is never what it seems with a class mid-field player and his facial expressions tell opponents nothing. In fact when he looks beaten and fed up, he is likely to be at his most dangerous, scheming a powerful re-entry into play. When the ball looks to be an easy pick-up, watch out for a razor-edged challenge from any class mid-field player. He may have appeared to have no chance and even less interest but with real mid-field maestros, appearances are always deceptive. . . very!!

5.11 Reading the Signs.

Most soccer players learn to read opponents' eyes and facial expressions, in fact all their movement mannerisms. Body language can be a reliable 'give away' with ordinary people, even with ordinary soccer players. Outstanding players, especially outstanding mid-field players, know how to send out totally false and yet convincing signs or 'vibes' if you like. Vibes which make 'reading' them extremely difficult. The time to catch them out, if it's possible, is when they are close to or better still actually involved in the action. When a player has to concentrate upon what he's doing, is the best time to know what his action options really are. Unless he's a truly great player he hasn't the time in which to practice deception. Having said that, the skill and sheer inventiveness of the great players. . . Gullitt of Holland, Baggio of Italy and in the recent past, Beckenbauer the German 'wunderspieler' who could even make doing the obvious deceptive. . . meant that they could put out false clues under the severest pressure from opponents.

Great soccer players, like great ball players in every sport, have to be outstanding actors and seeing, most definitely, is not necessarily believing in soccer.

5.2 Vision.

A mid-field player must have wide vision; the ability to see and remember what is happening in the most remote areas of the pitch. Vision enables him to select the most unlikely and distant targets for deceptive, effortlessly delivered long passes.

The ability to know what is going on everywhere on the pitch is a vitally important mid-field skill. Without it a player cannot have a true sense of the flow of play which every play controller needs.

Some years ago, when England's international fortunes went into serious decline, the country had probably the best long passer in the soccer world. Glen Hoddle of Tottenham Hotspur, Monaco in France and the current England team manager could drop the ball dead. . . or at least dying. . . at the feet of the fastest moving receiver anything up to sixty yards away. Diagram 28. And he could do it with little noticeable effort and absolutely no 'tell tale' signs worth the name. Hitting a wide and distant receiver with a long throw, as in American football, is kid stuff compared with hitting the same sort of target with your foot. . . and the receiver in soccer has to catch the ball and control it without using his hands!

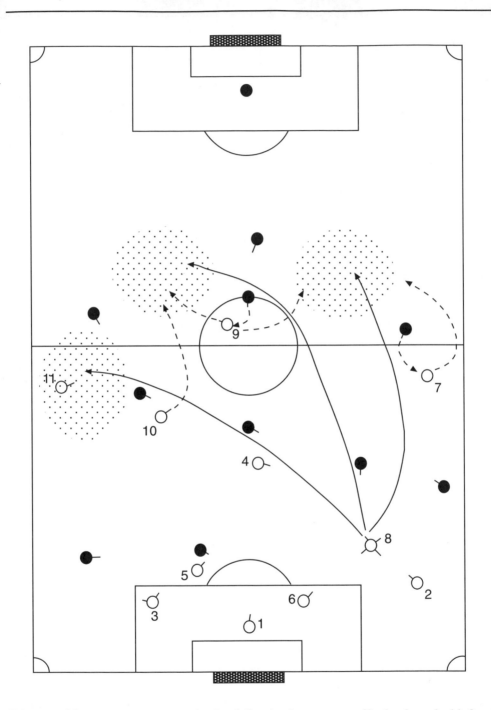

Diagram 28. Glen Hoddle's capacity for delivering long passes effortlessly and with few if any signals.

Hoddle was the Joe Montana of world soccer. . . but he wasn't picked for the England soccer team, at least not regularly. Of course, he wasn't the toughest or most tenacious player in pro-soccer but the world's great mid-field play-makers seldom are. Certainly Platini of France, Brazil's Rivellino and Di Stefano of Argentina. . . great mid-field orchestrators all. . . weren't expected to use muscle power when their brain power was so much more valuable.

The lesson is that if a player in a team has a supreme gift, use it.

Ordinary mid-field players are work horses: outstanding mid-field players are thoroughbreds.

5.3 Decoy Runs and Work Rate.

The exceptional mid-field player is never just a work horse. He must have the horse-power of a thoroughbred and he will be prepared to work at it. This means that he has to do a lot of running 'on' (with) and 'off' (without) the ball. 'Off the ball' runs are made when a player runs as if to receive a pass when his real purpose is to draw one or more defenders away from the player who is the real target for the passer. An out-standing 'off the ball' run is made when the runner can either receive a pass in a dangerous position or his run opens up the possibility for another receiver in an even better position. The passer has two options. Diagram 29.

'Off' the ball moves are sometimes called 'decoy' or 'dummy' runs because they are intended to attract the attention of opponents away from the true target of the playmaker. Because of his position in mid-field, especially in central mid-field, a player has opportunities to make decoy runs for back players wishing to play to other mid-field players or even direct to forwards. Diagram 30. He may make decoy runs for the advantage of other mid-field players and he may make them for the benefit of forward players. That's a lot of running!

In diagram 30, white mid-field players, 8 and 10, have made off the ball moves to draw defenders away from excellent target spaces for white 5 with the ball. White 10 's run is particularly clever because it has drawn a defender away from target space but he also offers the player with the ball a fine passing option as well. White 8 and 10 's runs have opened up mid-field space for white 5 should he see an oppor-tunity to run the ball deep into the opponents' half of the pitch.

In diagram 31 where the mid-field player, white 4, has the ball, two of the remain-ing three mid-field players have made very intelligent 'off the ball' runs. One, white 8, has gone on a 'loop' run behind and outside the player with the ball. If one or more of the defenders follow or even half follow his run, the path is open for the ball play-er to attack the space left. If the opponents don't cover white 8's run, he may receive a pass and will be able to attack the defense decisively. The second mid-field player, white 6, moving 'off the ball' and seeing the tactical move set up by his team mates, has moved forward and diagonally towards the central defenders thus opening up space and establishing white, 10, as a possible target player. The fourth player,

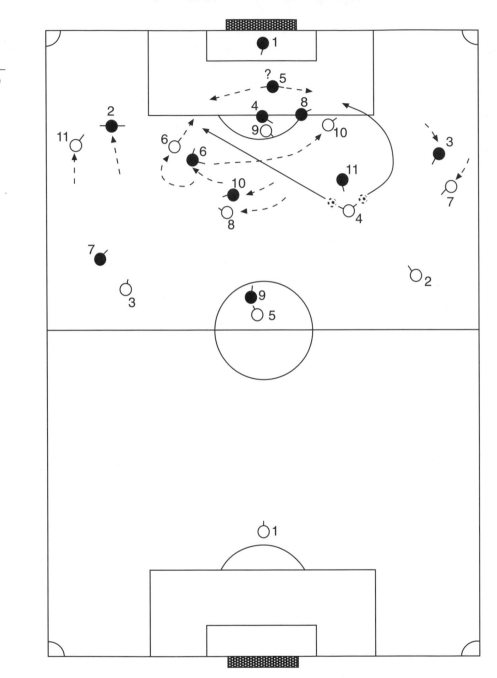

Diagram 29. Alternative passing options created by good 'off' the ball moves.

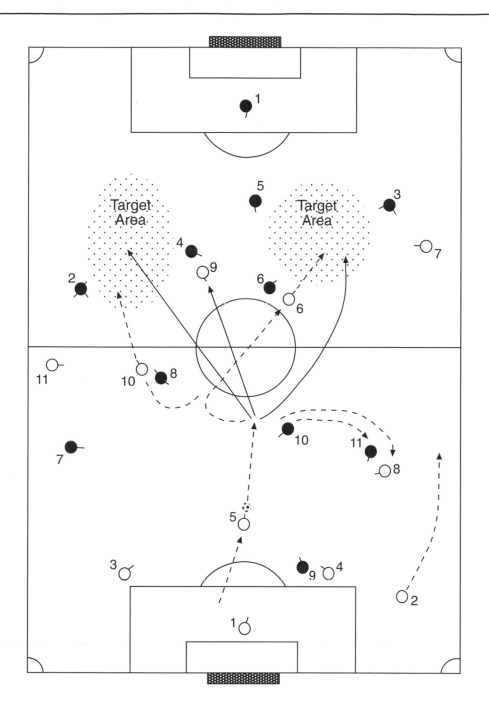

Diagram 30. Mid-field players make decoy runs. White 8 and 10 positive runs: White 6 to open up mid-field for back player white 5.

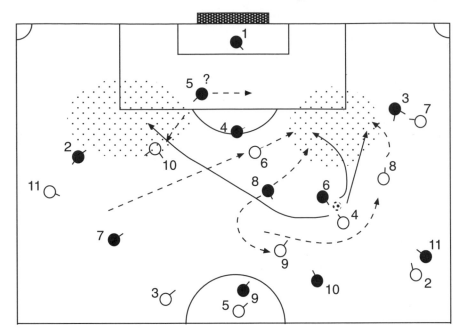

Diagram 31. Off the ball moves in attack close to the penalty area.

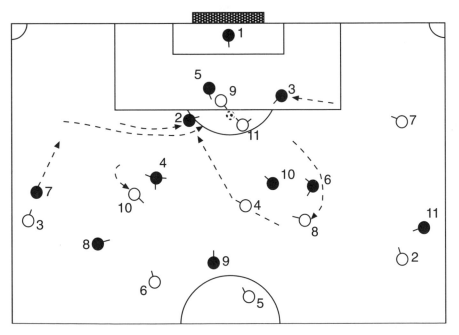

Diagram 32. A "passover" move near the penalty area showing the need for 'balancing' moves off the ball.

white 9, has assumed a covering and safe supporting position just in case the player with the ball is unable to accept any of the action options open to him.

In these examples of 'off the ball' moves, all the players are making them unselfishly for their mid-field colleagues.

In diagram 32 a pass has been played in to the feet of a central attacker, white 9. The wide attacker, white 11, has moved across field in front of white 9. He could receive a pass which might place him in a position to shoot instantly or with a second touch. White 4, his mid-field team mate, seeing the value of this move has moved aggressively and obviously towards the ball, probably shouting for a pass loudly. His intention is to attract the attention of defenders away from the more dangerous position into which white 11 is moving. These moves, to be successful need a great deal of practice and some very perceptive coaching in which the development of high levels of understanding and communication are the main aims. Poor coaches think that the mere repetition of the actions involved is the way that players learn best. They are poor because they don't know how to set up and direct realistic, effective learning situations; they become screamers!

It is my experience that the more that a coach shouts the less he is likely to know.

'Do as I say' coaching has little or nothing to offer to intelligent, skillful soccer players.

The basis for making effective decoy runs is the acceptance and the understanding by all the players of simple strategical objectives for different phases of play.

In diagram 33, where white 8, (and this could have been Glen Hoddle), has the ball let's assume that the team's attacking strategy is to switch play from wing to wing to try to unbalance opposing defenses. White 6 has made a sudden run at the space behind black 2. The run must be tracked by a defender. If the runner receives a pass the defense will have been breached. Here, the defender who must drop back is black 2.

In doing so he leaves the wing space available for white 11.

In similar circumstances and with practice, all players know that the decoy run has to be made with a good chance of a pass reaching that player if it becomes necessary.

'Dummy' runs made in the attacking quarter of the pitch are essential if teams are to stand any chance of exposing massed defenses. And they have to be made often.

In diagram 34, mid-field player white 8, has taken the chance to run the ball directly at the central defense. White 10 has moved quickly across his team mate's line of attack and in front of black 5 who must cover part of the run, at least until he's certain that another defender has picked up the runner. Even a three or four yard 'stretching effect' on the defenders' positional relationships, caused by the run, gives attackers the extra space and time needed to work a shot-producing move.

In diagram 35, the diagonal run of white 9 has been so well timed that his move in front of one defender and behind a second, has drawn (decoyed) both into following him. A scoring shot is inevitable in these circumstances. That particular move came off in a 1982 World Cup final match.

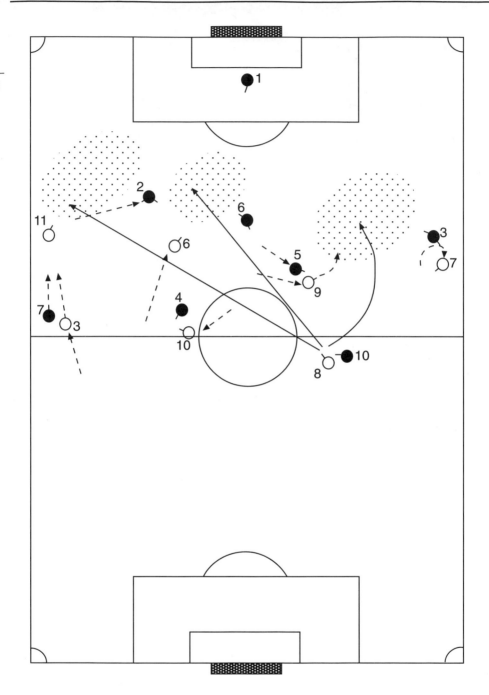

Diagram 33. Perceptive long passing 'off' the ball moves to create target spaces and options.

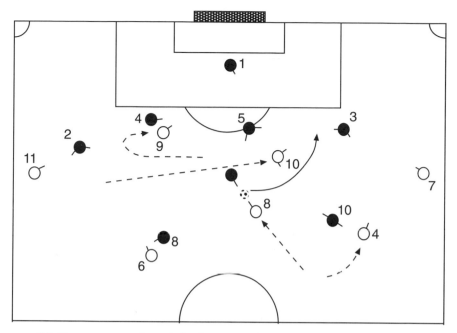

Diagram 34. Decoy runs to draw defenders away from prime targets.

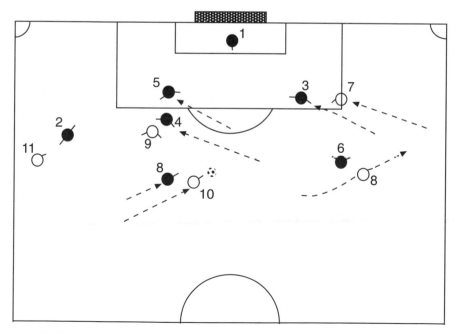

Diagram 35. Decoy runs need to be times to set unsolved marking and covering problems for defenders.

5.31 Loop (overlapping) Runs.

Overlapping runs are the curved runs made from behind or round the back of a player with the ball. The importance of (a) the path and (b) the timing of the run must be understood.

In diagram 36 the attacking team has moved the ball into it's opponents' half of the pitch without breaking through. There are still eight defenders and the goalkeeper in front of them; marking and covering is tight.

In diagram 36, the right central mid-field player, white 4 has moved behind and outside white 8, the player with the ball. His run sets problems for one perhaps even two defenders in the opposing team. If they move sideways to cover white 4's run, a gap will be opened through which white 8 can run the ball and link up with forward attackers. If white 4 times his run well he may also draw a covering move from the defender, black 5. Here, where there is a wide attacker in position, this attacker can help by making a diagonal, 'off the ball' run into centre field thus clearing the area for the overlapping run. All that is needed by the players is a clear understanding of the play's objectives. . . in this case, to 'turn' the wide defenders if possible.

An overlapping run from the position shown causes defenders to move sideways, movements which are necessary if an attacking team is to open up opposing defenses. Movements up and down the field only cause similar movements by defenders and don't create the space through which the ball can be passed or dribbled to greatest effect. Even so, where one player, positioned behind another player with the ball, diagram 37, can time his forward run as late as possible and achieve optimum surprise, the ball player's action options are increased significantly. He can pass to the forward running player; he can fake a pass and dribble forward or he can pass to another player enabling that player to link up with the loop runner. That's a lot of valuable options.

Strategies aimed at avoiding losing have caused the tactical 'fixing' of increasing numbers of players. Mid-field players nowadays may number three, four or even five, most of whom, in safety first teams, take up positional relationships with other players which rarely change. Their functions are strictly pre-programmed thereby reducing creativity to a minimum. The result. . . predictably. . . has been contests restricted to little more than one sixth of the total playing area available. Twenty highly trained athletes attempting to control the ball sensitively, to dribble or pass it precisely in an area as tight as that cannot make sense. . . and it doesn't!

Mid-field players restricted to eliminating each other leads to attritional, violent play, play which may appeal to soccer statisticians but which clearly doesn't appeal to spectators or, if the truth were known, to players. Professional managers and coaches, certainly in the game's mother country, England, have a lot to answer for. What they do today everyone. . . everyone with television and without imagination . . . copies tomorrow.

Mid-field players need freedom; freedom to make time and space in which to play; freedom to work out tactical options; freedom to interchange positions, to be

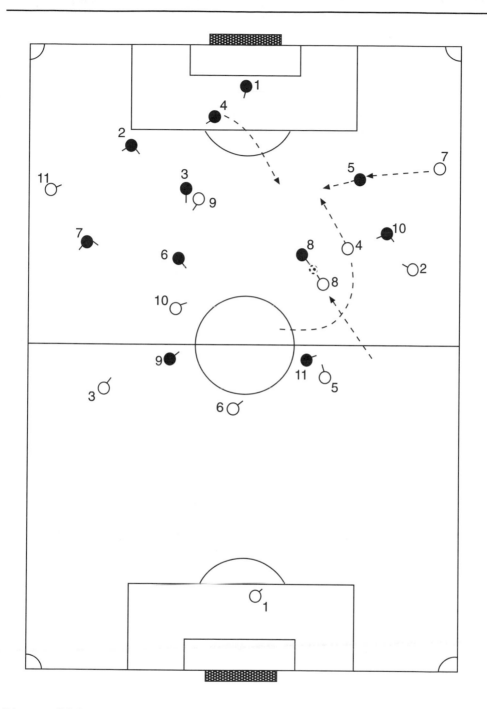

Diagram 36. Loop (overlapping) runs.

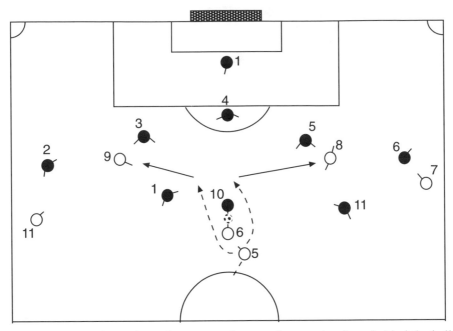

Diagram 37. Forward runs by a close supporting attacker moving from behind the ball carrier. Other attackers move wide to stretch the opposing defenders.

deceptively 'different' and so to pose difficult problems for opponents. They need freedom from the operational strait jackets which frightened coaches have compelled many of them to wear.

Attritional mid-field play, diagram 38, in which increasing numbers of players play to stop each other playing, is like trench warfare; a lot of energy is expended; the wounded increase in numbers but precious little progress is made!

Where a team's defensive strategy is to have at least nine, often more, players behind the ball as soon as opponents gain possession, space and time for individual or combined initiatives are at a premium. Back players and most mid-field players develop playing methods whereby they are never caught in positions from which they have to run hard or far to regain their required defensive stations.

'Once bitten twice shy' the proverb says and well meaning teams trying to play the game imaginatively but, angry at having been caught out by negative tactics, copy those methods next time round. The result is a majority of players and teams devoted exclusively to preventing each other from playing. English professional soccer has paid and continues to play a very high price for those methods.

The solution may be in the following.

5.4 Fluid Positional Play.

Tactical inflexibility of the kind described leads to soccer nonsense, to crippling stagnation in fact.

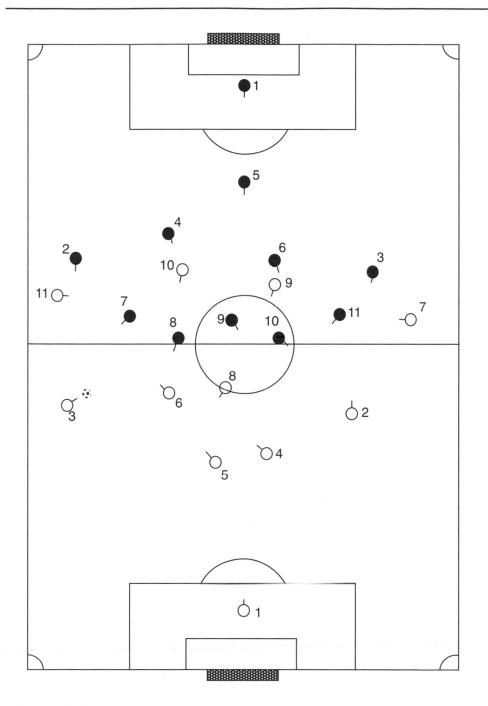

58

Diagram 38. Mass retreat to deep defense.

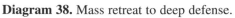

If the only reason for playing the game is to avoid losing by preventing opponents from playing, there is no point in playing at all. The game played this way is neither entertaining for those watching nor interesting for those playing.

One solution is to allow mid-field players to make space and time by interchanging positions freely whenever their team has the ball. Interchanging positions offers a player with the ball different and changing action options. It also compels movement by opposing defenders who have to track, cover and generally react to the moves of their opponents. Positional interchange in attack should be totally free, indeed it should be required of all young players. Only by trying different moves will they find out which moves enable team mates to pass the ball to them easily and safely and which make the defenders' problem more difficult. Trial and error becomes trial and success. Some moves will be 'discovered' to set extremely difficult problems for opponents; others have no effect on opponents whatsoever.

Good coaches set up practice situations in which players always have two or more choices for action. As players experiment with different solutions imaginative coaches guide them towards the most profitable options. Of course, if the coach doesn't know which options ARE the most profitable then the game and the players have serious problems.

Answers to soccer problems cannot be simply right or wrong. There are always a number of action options for any single player and for the players with whom he is trying to play.

5.41 Cross-over Moves.

In diagram 39, where white 5 has the ball, other mid-field players are balancing different cross-over moves one against the other. As one mid-field player makes a forward diagonal run, into a space perhaps, a team mate runs in the opposite direction. They are trying to 'stretch' defenders and throw off markers. Depending on the timing of each run, one or the other may escape his marker and receive the ball. Timing is everything in making positive runs. Those who know soccer well regard this skill as one of the hallmarks of true class. The secret of good timing depends on each player having a clear understanding of attacking priorities and what each is trying to do.

In the defensive half of the field, a player making the forward run will start his run first. If he moves clear of his opponent and the target space towards which he is running is comfortably within the ball player's passing range, the pass will go to him. Having seen his team mate begin his forward run, the player making the counter-move, towards the ball player, will start his run when he is confident that his team mate has escaped from his marker. If he has, the countermove will be made suddenly and as late as possible. Delaying the countermove means that a marker will not have time to judge which move to cover. The forward run is more threatening but the counter run may free the player for whom that marker is responsible. By the time he has sorted out his priorities a defender will be able to cover neither. The ball player will have a good forward moving target, white 8 or 6 in diagram 39, but if he

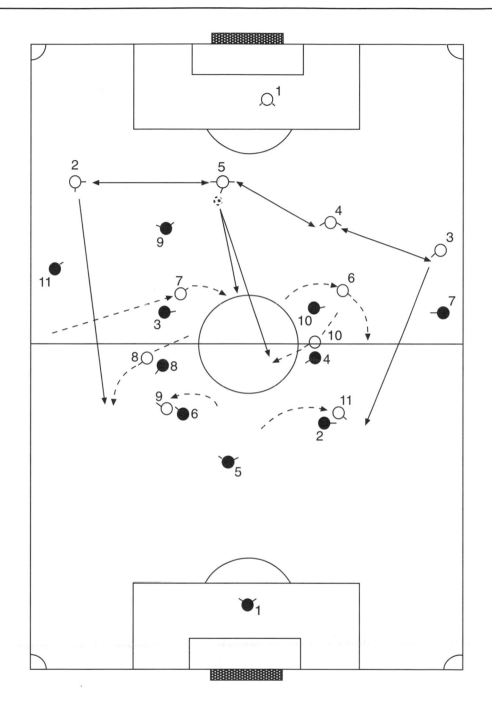

Diagram 39. Cross over interchanges by white mid-fielders and good forward passing options.

has the slightest doubt he has the absolutely safe target, white 7, coming to meet his pass.

In the attacking half of the pitch, diagram 40, the player moving to meet the player with the ball makes the first move. This is because the primary target for a pass is a forward moving player, white 9 or 11. . . if they are in a team trying to score goals! Well timed interchanges and cross-over runs are essential if players are to break the mid-field 'log jam' which prevails in so many countries today.

In teams which use cross-over moves successfully, one player is always the 'trigger'; the other player, or players, time their moves 'off' him.

In diagram 41, where white 10 has few worthwhile forward options, he has turned to 'hide' the ball by showing his back to the nearest opponent. Mid-field player, white 8, runs close behind his team mate and according to a pre-arranged signal either takes the ball or pretends to take it but leaves it for white 10 to spin away into space. The two black defenders have been drawn into the same confined space but neither knows which attacker is likely to make the break with the ball from the cross-over position.

If the players crossing over stay tight to each other, defenders can't really see what is happening. Sideways and forward moves with and without the ball are essential if attacking teams are to expose deep zonal defenses. Sideways moves attract sideways reactions from opponents which tend to create spaces through which passes can be delivered and collected.

Mid-field players, as we have already seen, are best placed of all the players to 'use' other players to develop fluid team movement in attack. Fundamental to understanding the action principles involved is knowing the probability of certain actions and reactions occurring. For example, when faced by a player who plays the ball past him, especially towards goal, a defender almost certainly will turn his head to see where the ball has gone. He becomes, if only for a split second, a 'ball watcher'. Ball watchers cannot be player watchers. . . at least not easily. It is when an opponent's attention has been drawn elsewhere that the passing player moves for a return pass. If the defender has turned his head to look behind and over his right shoulder, the attacker moves past his left shoulder and vice versa. He should always move in the direction opposite to the turn of the defender's head unless he deliberately seeks to attract the defender's attention of course. The opponent may not immediately turn to look for the ball, be patient. . . he will!

If the passing player slows down the action until, at the time when he gives the pass, he and his immediate opponent are almost standing still, he will win any short sprint to receive a return pass if only because he starts the race!

5.42 Pendulum Passing.

To make a pendulum pass the passer follows his own pass to receive a return pass into space at one side or the other of the player to whom he originally passed the ball. Diagram 42. The return pass may be immediate, i.e. with one touch, or delayed, i.e. with two or more touches. Pendulum passes are used to set up good inter-passing

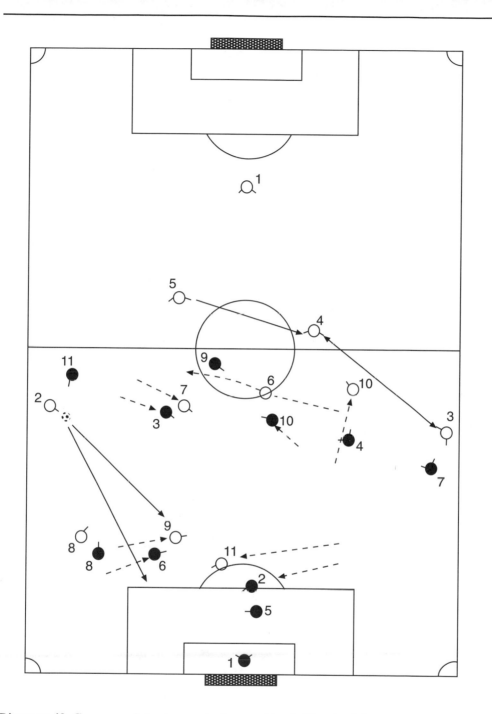

Diagram 40. Cross over interchanges in the attacking half maintaining team shape.

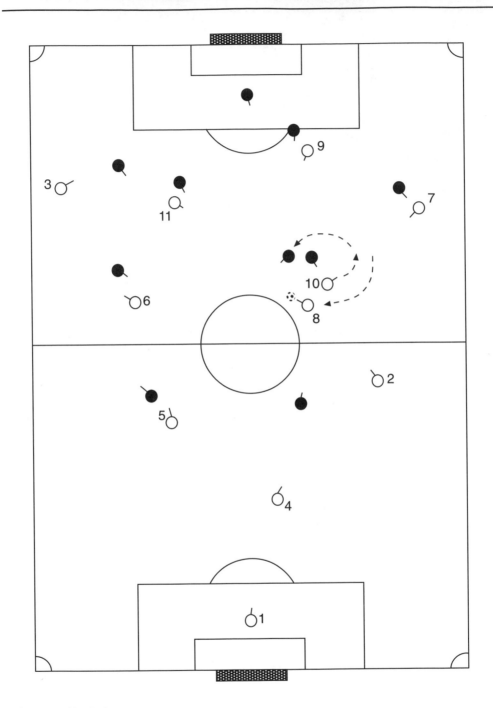

Diagram 41. Tight cross over moves.

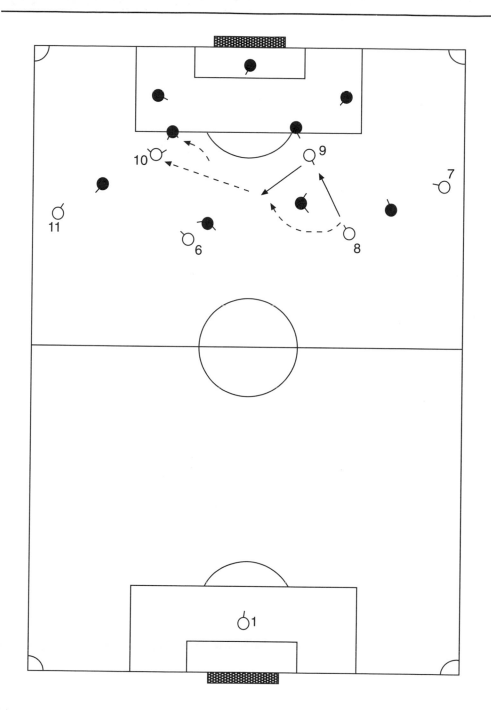

Diagram 42. Pendulum Passes.

angles to exploit two against one situations often where free space is nearly non-existent. They are particularly effective near to or within the penalty area where the return pass often produces a shooting opportunity close in and central to the goal.

In diagram 42, mid-field player white 8, has given a forward pass to the feet of striker white 9. Waiting for his opponent's attention to be drawn by the ball, he moves past him for a return pass 'laid off' along the line down which he is moving. Knowing his team mate's intention, he must be prepared to shoot first time.

In diagram 43, the central striker moves sideways to take his marker out of the space into which he intends to lay off the pendulum pass. The mid-field player plays his setting up pass into unoccupied space making sure that the striker can reach the ball before any defender while drawing his marker with him.

In diagram 44 where the same basic move has been set up, the player setting up the play is too far from the striker to stand any chance of reaching a first touch return pass before an opponent. White 10, who is nearer to the action moves to receive the pass instead: he may shoot or play a through pass to white 7, who has now moved beyond the striker anticipating that possibility.

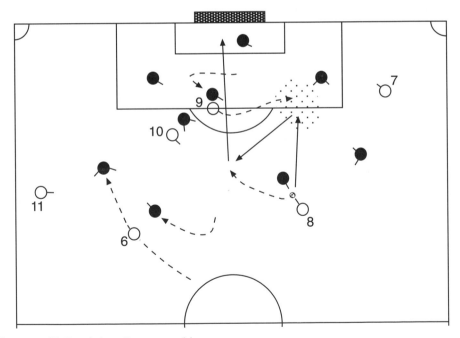

Diagram 43. Pendulum Passes: making space.

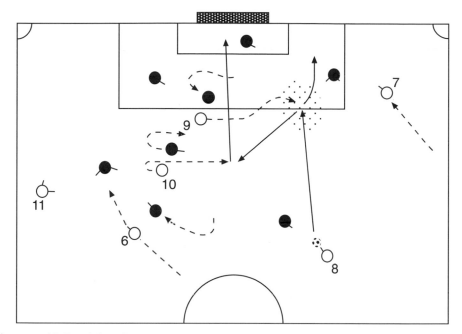

Diagram 44. Pendulum Pass.

5.43 'Third Man' Moves.

This is known as 'third man' play because, in any situation involving interpassing possibilities between three players, the 'third' or least immediately involved player must always seek to receive passes forward of the other two.

Diagram 45 shows three players playing against three in practice. When one player passes to another, those two players are to a certain extent fixed by their actions: they are doing something. . . passing or receiving. . . which takes time and attention. The third player has a choice: he can stop where he is, which may cause the move to come to a standstill, or he can move to give the other players a forward passing option if the possibility occurs.

The third man will not always be the same player. In diagram. 45 (c), the player giving the first pass has moved to receive the return pass. The 'third man' is now white B, who must 'show himself' in a more advanced position if the attack is to go forward. Any one of the three players finding himself briefly out of the passing move, must look for another position in advance of play. This is why all attacking moves need at least three players if supporting positions are to be set up from which penetrating passing moves can develop.

This is not to say that two players can't be successful in penetrating a defense: it is to say that a third player improves the range of options enormously. The third player. . . and the fourth if there is one nearby. . . must move ahead, and no 'ifs' or 'buts': whatever they may or may not finally achieve, forward 'runs' draw defenders away from space desperately needed by mid-field attackers trying to set up accurate attacking moves.

It is absolutely essential for a mid-field player. . . and a sound idea for all players . . . having given a pass to move to another position. Where? Preferably where he can receive a return pass to shoot or to carry the movement forward towards the shooting area. If such positive moves aren't on, then he should move to draw opponents out of positions in which they might block other players' forward moves. If mid-field players pass and stand still, opposing players stand with them. Where a team has four players in mid-field, all of whom want to pass but not move, those four in fact become eight; the four mid-field players plus four opponents.

'Third Man' moves were the basis of the elegant, ground passing style known as 'Push and Run' at Tottenham Hotspur F. C. in England and fundamental to the intricate, short interpassing game of the Austrian Wundermannschaft in the nineteen forties.

5.5 Clearing Space.

Drawing opponents away from play to make space is a subtle skill. Playing against opponents committed to strict man-to-man defense it is relatively easy because markers, usually, will track opponents wherever they go.

Against 'heavy' zone defense, diagram 46, drawing opponents away from important space requires a clear understanding by the attackers of how defenders think and operate. Before attackers can make sense of difficult defensive problems, they need

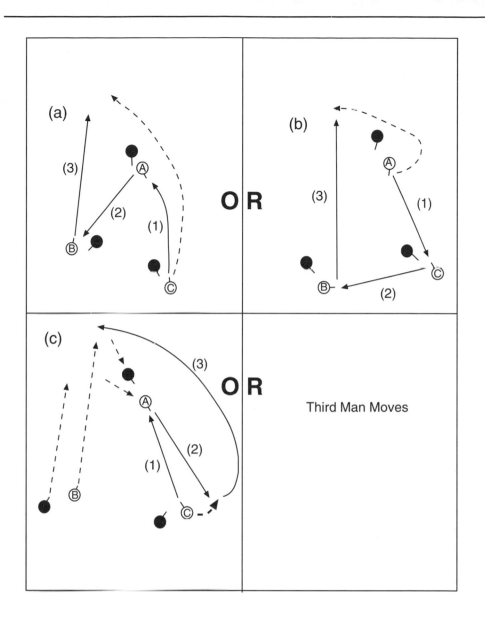

Diagram 45.

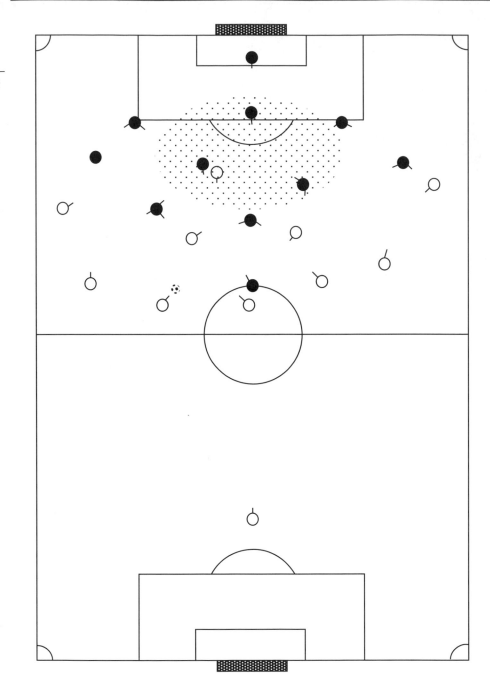

Diagram 46. Heavy zone defense.

to know what defenders are trying to do and what defenders' reactions to certain attacking moves are likely to be. Obviously the reverse is true for defenders.

In diagram 46 too many white players are in negative positions. They may guarantee long periods of ball possession but they will hardly cause a ripple of concern among the defending side. In diagram 47 where there are still three 'fail safe' players outside their opponents' defensive set up, there are now five players well inside it and a sixth who could quickly become an inside attacker. Those six players must be marked tightly wherever they go inside the defense and so they begin to exert control over their opponents. Understanding the enemy is more than half the battle: that's why poachers make the best game-keepers.

Sound knowledge of defensive principles, acute awareness of what defenders' action options are and a general sense of the likely pattern of play are essential for successful attacking play. The most perceptive players develop a sense of how and where play is likely to develop. It comes from a general awareness of the positions and movements of different players, much like the sense developed by the experienced car driver who 'senses' when trouble is likely without appearing to watch the actions of every other driver on the road. In fact that's precisely what he does but so quickly that it seems like instinct. It isn't.

This isn't a sense in the true meaning of the word it is a learned skill. And it is important that soccer teachers and coaches realize the difference. Without this awareness, a player will be seriously handicapped at the higher levels of play.

Good soccer players are continuously receiving and processing information about space, about options and about other players.

Non-stop play demands non-stop thinking.

Acute game awareness is common to all the perpetual motion games like Basketball, Field Hockey and Soccer. In stop and start games like American Football, Baseball and Rugby a game sense is needed by a limited number of players especially where the game is played within highly controlled patterns. And the perpetual motion games' players definitely make the best car drivers!

Where mid-field players, tracked and marked closely, sense possibilities for a counter attack led by one or both central defenders, they ease casually into positions wide of the anticipated direction of attack. They hold wide positions briefly in case the back players need them as supporting players or even to transfer the attack to them. If the backs go on, the mid-field players let them pass and drift into covering positions behind them. Effectively the backs are temporary attacking mid-field players and the midfielders are temporary centre backs.

Opponents must follow the moves of the mid-field players or let them go free. If they block the central attacking drive they leave the mid-field players in positions from which they can keep the attack moving forward.

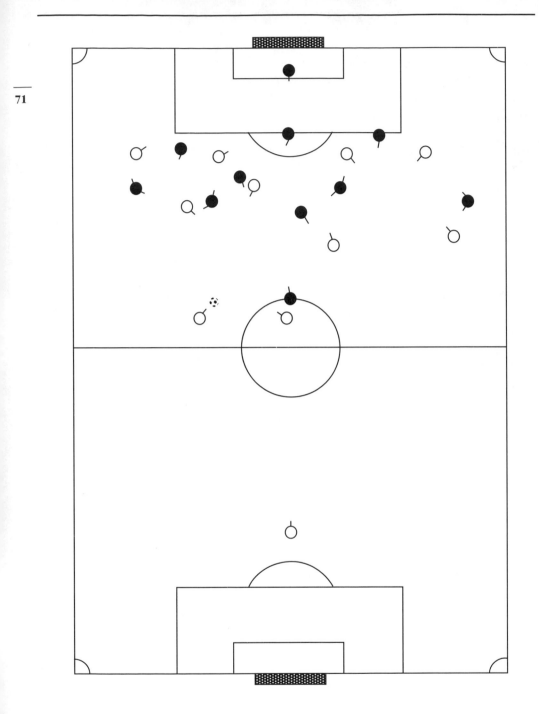

Diagram 47.

5.51 'Outside In' and 'Inside Out' Moves.

A basic defensive principle is that defenders. . . good ones that is. . . track closely any moves from wide to central: particularly those towards the most profitable shooting areas. Moves from central to wide positions occasion less concern. Tracking moves by defenders from 'inside' positions to 'outside', tends not to be so close and more relaxed.

An attacker stands a better chance of escaping his marker moving from inside positions outwards but he is more likely to take an opponent with him when he moves from outside positions inwards.

These are tactical probabilities but not certainties.

If drawing an opponent is the important objective, a mid-field player indicates his intention, by shouting for a pass perhaps, and by threatening to run behind the defender before running in front of him. Defenders 'switch on' when attackers shout for the ball. Which is why an intelligent player moving to receive a pass in a good position, to shoot say, rarely if ever shouts. Defenders are likely to be alerted by any player shouting for the ball as he tries to move behind them towards goal.

If receiving the ball is the main consideration, a player is more likely to be allowed to receive it moving from inside to out. His move should be made at an easy, non-threatening pace so that there is no element of surprise. Surprise moves made quickly tend to alert or frighten opponents and alert opponents react quickly.

As the potential target player moves wide he waits for the moment when his opponent relaxes from a tight marking to a tracking movement. The defender is saying, in effect, that the attacker is moving into an area which the defender doesn't consider to be immediately dangerous. At that point the attacker slows down or even stops because to go any further, almost certainly, would find him picked up by another defender. Diagram 48. Whatever moves he makes from this point will be aimed at keeping the same amount of space between himself and defenders and therefore at giving himself the optimum space in which to receive a pass. In today's soccer at the top level, where space is so difficult to find, it is important that all players but especially mid-field players give themselves the maximum space possible in which to play.

In attack, all forward and midfield players must prepare for the possibility of the ball arriving all the time. Attackers must search for those positions which are at the limit of their opponent's immediate concern. In top class soccer that may mean no more than an extra two yards of freedom; matches are won and lost on that amount of freedom close to goal.

Attacking and supporting players must continuously test the concern of their opponents; to do so may require sustained movements, into, through and to the fringe of the key shooting areas, often for substantial periods of play. Adjusting position to gain another two or three square yards has to be continuous. Without this sort of concentrated determination, a mid-field player will find it extremely difficult if not

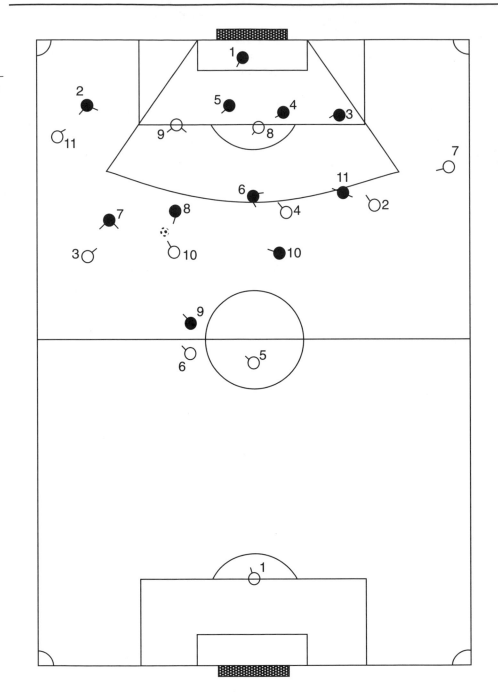

Diagram 48. 'Inside out' moves.

impossible to get into the game.

In the opposing penalty area, without this acute sense of space and the sense of timing which enables a player to move undetected often, attackers gain few if any goal scoring positions.

Mid-field players, opposed by large numbers of opponents, must develop space awareness enabling them to see one, two or three moves ahead. This sense enables them to move easily and unhurriedly into position often well ahead of play.

Occasionally players have to move into negative spaces, spaces which don't promote attacking play and in which they are of little use to the player on the ball. They do this to 'soften up' defensive attention.

Great players, even without the ball, cause more trouble for opponents than ordinary players do with it. They have the ability to receive the ball or to move into effective space, without causing the slightest concern. They compel defenders to worry and to continually ask themselves,

"Why is he going there?"

"Should I go with him or stay?"

"If he gets the ball can I control him?"

"If I follow him, is he taking me for 'a ride'?" and so on.

High class attackers are always testing their opponents' thinking and acting speeds.

5.52 'Fixing' opponents.

Occasionally it's necessary to 'fix' opponents, to persuade them to stand still in a certain area or to restrict their ability to move where and when they choose. All teams, from time to time, have certain players who are outstanding in certain aspects of the game. For example a skillful, play-making mid-field player may find himself marked by an opponent intent solely on putting him out of the game, one way or another!

Sacrificing one ordinary player to eliminate an outstanding opponent may be a good deal for most coaches.

The mid-field player tries every trick in the book. . . even in this book. . . but the opponent is a 'sticker'. Clearly tactics have to be devised to break his concentration. The marked player may simply stand still in the middle of the field and other than being used as a rebound wall for team mates' passes, he may allow play to pass him by in all directions. It is a great test of a player's will to mark an opponent who refuses to move in any direction. Both players will look slightly ridiculous but which player will lose patience first? The marker may be 'conned' into thinking that his opponent has given up but if he tries to assume a normal part in the game, he may find his opponent running free: he may be difficult to pick up again.

Alternatively the player marked may reverse his role and mark the opponent! Sounds impossible? Think about it. What will a man-for-man marker do if the player he is marking assumes all the attitudes of a marker himself? Whatever else happens I'll guarantee that one of the players is puzzled.

A mid-field player marked out of the game may choose to move into one of the back defenders' positions, taking his marker with him. As he does so, a back exchanges position by moving into mid-field. Again the marked mid-field player has reversed roles with his opponent: the marker is now marked and one team has a free player in mid-field.

This role reversal tactic is easily achieved when a team plays with a sweeper or free back. Without a free back, the defense may find itself without a spare player when the opposing team counter attacks.

5.6 Group tactics in defense.
5.61 Splitting opponents.
When defending, mid-field players must be good judges of the distance they can afford to leave between themselves and the opponents for whom they have containing or challenging responsibilities.

In diagram 49, a back defender is counter-attacking through centre field at speed. The nearest opposing, mid-field player, white 10, must contain the counter-attacker and deflect him away from centre field. To do this he has to concede a degree of freedom to black 10, who has drawn away from him.

White's priorities are clear, he must check the opponent's run but he must also be able to move to contain the next move should black 10 receive the ball. He has to 'split' his responsibilities between the two opponents threatening to penetrate his defensive zone.

In diagram 50, three mid-field players are 'splitting' four opponents. If they each understand what the team's tactics are aimed at achieving, they stand a good chance of succeeding. For example, the tactics might be to persuade opposing mid-field players to play towards centre field rather than wide towards the touch-lines. The defending team might need to gain interceptions in parts of the pitch which would give them the best platform for a counter attack, if they were losing with not long to play for example. Alternatively, tactics might be to compel opponents to play out-wards, from centre field, towards the wings. Tactical awareness of weaknesses among the central back players identifies the need to prevent opponents from attacking those weaknesses, i.e. centrally.

Either way, as each mid-field player begins to close down (reduce) the space between himself and an opponent with the ball, he will do so from an angle which guides his opponent in the required direction.

Players must know what their tactical objectives are in any phase of the game. Half the team playing to no tactical plan. . . or failing to remember what it is. . . makes no sort of sense, but it happens, even in the highest reaches of the game.

5.62 Giving Ground. (Retreating)
Where defending mid-field players are outnumbered, they need to know how to 'give ground' in front of an attack: to retreat while retaining significant control over the opposing attackers. Control is needed to deflect opponents towards areas in which

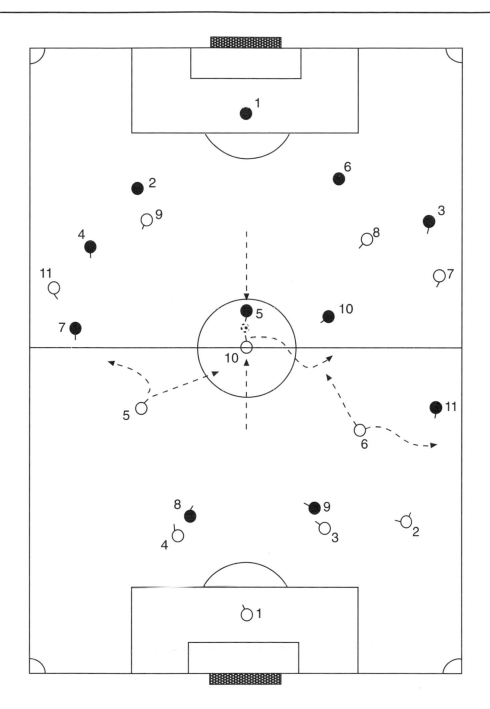

Diagram 49. Splitting opponents.

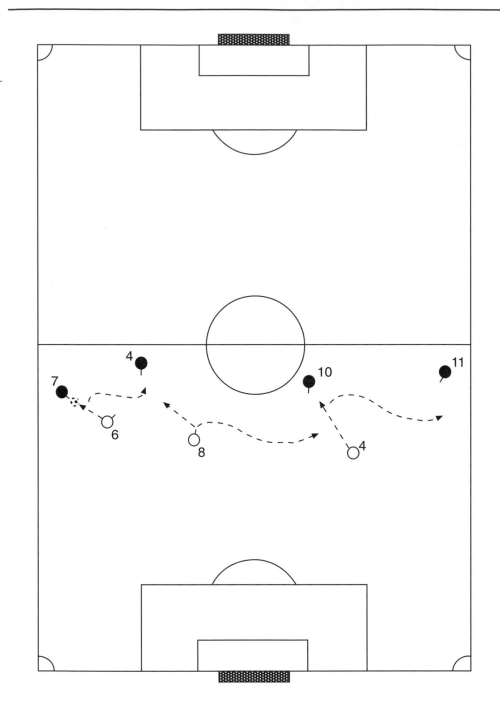

Diagram 50. Three splitting four.

numerical superiority can be canceled out. Retreat can be passive or active.

Passive retreat is used when the defender's speed. . . reaction and movement. . . is sufficient enough to counter opponents' moves to run or dribble past him. In other words the defending player can afford to wait for the opponent to make a mistake knowing, almost certainly that he will.

Active retreat is used when the defender feels that allowing his opponent to take the initiative gives the opponent too much of an advantage. The defender may be aware of an opponent's superior pace or outstanding trickiness with the ball. To control the action he must force his opponent into options that, given time, the opponent would not normally choose. This is called 'working' or 'pressurizing' an opponent.

Individual defensive skills will be used according to certain agreed priorities, depending on where and how the need occurs and on the state of the game. A team losing one goal to nil, with five minutes remaining, will defend differently from a team winning one to nil at the same stage of play. At least I hope that it will!

5.63 'Trapping' or 'Boxing in'.

The objective is to persuade opposing attackers:
    (a) to play in a predictable direction
    (b) to move the ball into an area from which they will have difficulty in developing further attacking movements.
    (c) to isolate key attackers so that they either give the ball away or they are dispossessed.

    (a) should lead to (b) and in turn to (c).

The first requirement of the defending player is to persuade his opponent to keep the ball until he can only pass in a direction which suits the defending players! If the attacker does pass, he must be encouraged to pass the ball negatively, to players who are no better positioned than he is, preferably worse.

Having confronted an opponent in possession, the defender must position himself to make the attacker choose to move sideways. This will depend upon,
    • the relative speed of each player,
    • the sureness of the attacker's ball control ,
    • his ability to make 'feint' moves successfully,
    • and the availability of other attackers to offer the ball player inter-passing options.

These factors will be affected by the location of the action on the field of play. An attacker with the ball is likely to be more aggressive and positive the nearer he is to the opposing goal. He is also more likely to take risks with the ball. Near to his own goal he may be apprehensive about making mistakes and therefore cautious. These are important considerations for defenders.

To 'trap' an opponent with the ball, the defender must approach him at an angle so that the attacker has no choice other than to move away from the defender and preferably towards a sideline. Diagram 51.

As the attacker moves in the required direction, the defender tightens up the angle; he squeezes his opponent in the required direction. The defender must be alert for any attempt by the attacker to twist and turn in the opposite direction: that may be the time to tackle. The defending midfielder must not open his positional angle too much. The attacker may accept the opening if he has the speed to get through it.

If the team tactical objective is to trap all the relevant attackers in a 'dead' area, the midfield defender will offer any player with the ball certain pre-arranged and very limited passing options, preferably one. Nearby co-defenders will also encourage the ball player to accept their opponents as pass options knowing that if they are accepted, the attacking team is in even worse trouble. Diagram 52. That is the time when defenders will step up pressure to regain possession of the ball or knock it out of play.

Throw-ins enable a well organized team to continue to apply a tactical squeeze nevertheless they give opponents possession of the ball in conditions which may be to their advantage. With the throw in, opponents can control what will happen and even more importantly when it will happen, within limits.

Generally speaking, forward players begin the tactical deflection whereby opponents' attacking play is induced to move in predictable directions and thereby contained in tight areas. According to tactical pre-arrangements, mid-field players offer an opening to the trap and then apply the squeeze to persuade (or force) play into areas from which free attacking play is impossible. Back players, of course work to offer the opposing ball player no forward outlets at all. The emphasis has to be on work since entrapment brings about a two way struggle. It also requires considerable tactical patience by the mid-field unit. They show opponents the trap-door and they close it.

5.64 Pressure Points. (Nose Defenders)
In active defense, defenders try to force opponents into making errors. Where opposing backs, say, have broken through the early containment by the forwards, one of the mid-field players must provide the advanced point of defensive pressure and resistance.

As the ball is transferred from one attacker to another, each probing for a defensive weakness, a defending mid-field player, supported by the players on each side of him, moves forward towards the ball and becomes what can be described. . . for obvious reasons. . . as the nose defender. Diagram 53. He creates a pressure point aimed at deflecting attacking threats sideways away from centre field. His objective is to persuade the player on the ball to choose wide passing options rather than forward (and more dangerous) angles. The supporting players move forward to cover the 'nose' defender and to urgently pressurize the passing options available on either side of him. Some teams use the same player as the 'nose' defender across most of the central attacking front. Following the transference of the ball, he 'shepherds' opposing play sideways until the ball has been moved well over to the side of the

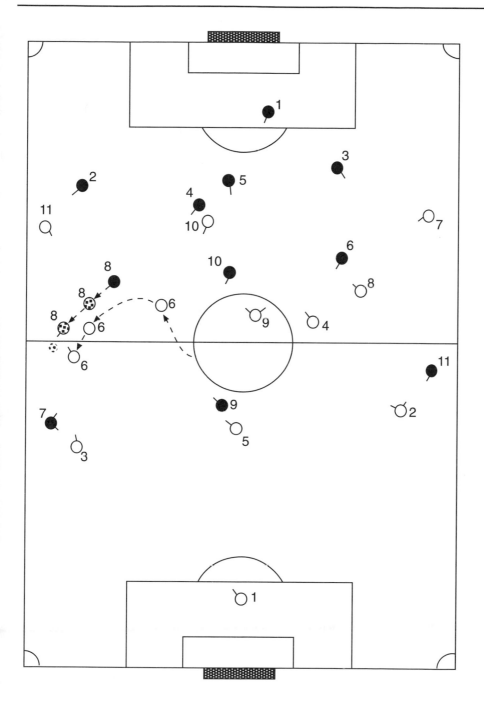

Diagram 51. Trapping or Boxing in.

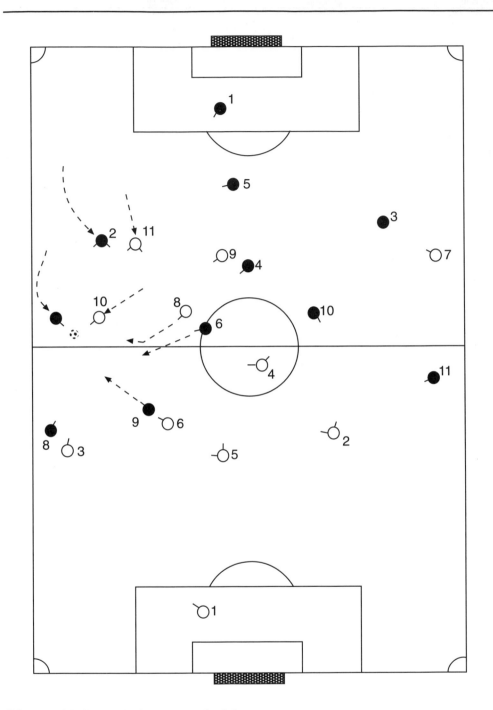

Diagram 52. 'Squeezing' opponents in tight areas.

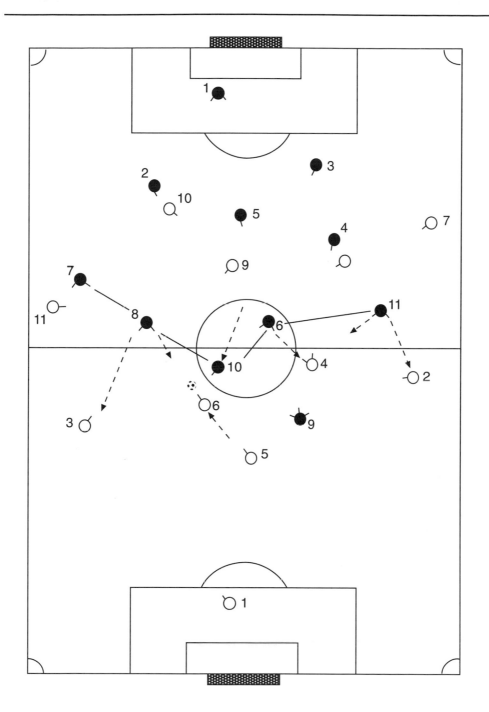

Diagram 53. The 'nose' defender pressurizes to deflect the ball player.

pitch. As attackers are guided towards the side-line, defenders use that line to squeeze the already limited area from which the attackers are trying to escape and thereby increase the pressure on them. Diagrams 51 and 52 previously. Defenders then close in around their opponents and actively challenge for the ball.

Defenders who stand and wait for opponents to run the ball at them, dribbling and inter-passing, will find that they are only too willing to seize the opportunity.

Some teams committed to heavy numerical defense and having deflected play into wide and safer areas, may tempt an attacker with the ball to penetrate the mid-field curtain. He is then surrounded by opponents cutting off any movement or passing escape outlet; much like the spider's use of his web. Diagram 54. As we have seen elsewhere, this was the basis of the famous and highly effective Italian 'curtain defense'.

Curtain defense requires expert calculation by mid-field defenders of the extent to which they can permit an opponent, with the ball, to penetrate the primary defensive curtain. He may be quick and clever enough to burst through the first 'curtain' of defenders and beyond the second as well.

Defense is cat and mouse play but not all 'mice' are stupid. . . at least in Soccer they aren't!

5.7 Individual Tactical Skills

Individual players have their own tactical skills. These personal tactics may or may not involve the use of technical skills. For example, a defender may wish to test an opponent's technical skill in bringing a pass under control. Tactically, he may move or threaten to move very quickly in the opponent's direction even when a pass to that player is only a remote possibility. He is warning his opponent that should a pass be given, the opponent can expect little if any time in which to control the pass before coming under severe challenge. The defender creates doubts in the mind of his opponent and thereby gains tactical advantage. Whenever the attacker looks at his opponent, he will find that opponent watching him, often with a superior, confident smile or with mean aggression on his face. This is legal intimidation; it should be taught and practiced.

The attacker can use personal tactical skill to counter the threat by the defender. Putting on an expression of submission to the defender's threat, he will move about as if beaten before the ball is anywhere near him. Then he may move, suddenly and very quickly, towards play. His intention will not be to get involved in actual play but to show his marker how quickly and surprisingly he can move, when necessary. He is showing his opponent that, in order to intercept a pass or to make the threatened early challenge for the ball, the defender must be prepared to move equally quickly into unfamiliar areas of the pitch.

All the problems in soccer have answers and they are to be found inside players' and coaches' heads, not outside them.

A personal tactical skill is used to disconcert an opponent and thereby to gain psychological advantage over him.

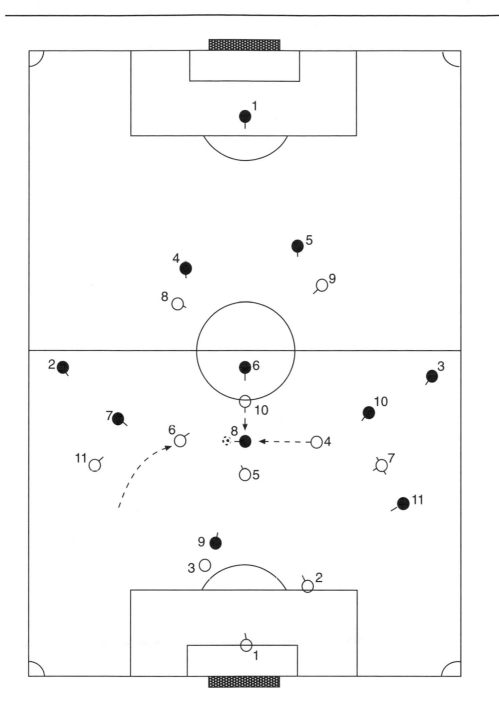

Diagram 54. *Catenacchio.*

5.71 Attack: Running with the Ball.

A mid-field player has the important responsibility for linking defense with attack and of playing a key role in each. Traditionally, linkage was established through the mid-field player's superior ball playing ability and through his superior stamina. He, of all the players, was expected to cover the most ground while exercising the highest levels of ball skill. Mid-field players in the old days were in every sense exceptional players.

Studies carried out in England thirty years ago showed mid-field players covering more than 6,000 yards during a match, much of that distance, about 4,000 yards, while striding if not actually sprinting but of course executing all the skills expected of a soccer player at the same time. The remaining 2,000 yards, approximately, were covered at high speed, often flat out sprinting and still involved in applying the game's skills effectively. Today, while it is highly unlikely that the total distance covered has increased, the distance covered at speed may be nearer to 2,500 yards.

In the context of a highly skillful sport, including the probability of body contact between players , that represents a great deal of very hard work. To maintain high levels of technical precision and tactical perception, indicates the intensity of training and practice needed to enable a first-class mid-field player to remain competitive at the top level. And to some extent all players in modern soccer are becoming mid-field players. . . at least in the all round competence and commitment expected from them.

A mid-field player is expected to be an accurate long and short passer but he can best exercise the element of surprise when, instead of passing, he runs or dribbles the ball powerfully and cleverly at and past opponents. That's how he always has a tactical edge.

Mid-field players MUST develop strength and skill when running with the ball. Opponents are never quite sure how to handle a mid-field player able to mix passing options with powerful dribbling options.

Additionally, when faced by a mid-field player with known ability to run with the ball, opponents are likely to stand off such a player to give themselves space in order to steal his space before he can run into it. Or so they think. Standing 'off' the mid-field player allows him that extra time and space in which to assess and to exploit his alternative, passing options.

5.72 Get Lost.

In modern 'pro' soccer the mid-field zone is about ten to twenty yards deep and may occupy no more than fifty yards of the full width of the pitch. In that area, eight or more players from each team contest every move and counter move skillfully and fiercely. When their team is in possession of the ball, most mid-field players are expected to struggle for forward positions behind their mid-field opponents and towards the opponents' goal. Diagram 55. The opposing mid-field players struggle equally strongly to deny their opponents these positions.

To break the deadlock mid-field players must know how to get lost: how to lose their markers. In diagram 56, where the white team has won the ball, one mid-field player, white 6, has 'drifted' out of mid-field temporarily into a position in line with his central backs. He has done this for a number of tactical reasons. If his move attracts an opponent then he has given the other mid-field players more space in which to play. There are now two fewer players occupying the congested space in mid-field.

If his move doesn't attract a counter-move by an opponent, he has still made more space but he has left his mid-field unit outnumbered by one in their mid-field contest. Where there are three against four, this will not matter so much; especially if, by tactical prearrangement, any one of the back players is free to replace him in supporting mid-field developments.

Alternatively, the 'drifter' may move backwards and away from the action and then round the side into a half-way forward position. Diagram 56. Of course an opponent may track his move but the result is more space for the remaining mid-field contestants and the possibility now of additional support for the forwards should the mid-field contest be won, however briefly, by his team mates.

Some years ago Belgium became a highly rated European soccer nation partly on the ability of its biggest and most recognizable player, Jan Ceulemans, to become invisible!

Ceulemans would literally disappear from mid-field or defensive action and reappear in advanced forward and goal scoring positions. He did the disappearing trick by being seen to involve himself as a supporting player in the development of Belgian mid-field interpassing movements. When he saw that his team mates could control ball possession safely without him, he stood still and allowed play to pass him by. Drawn by the magnetism of the ball, opponents tended to lose sight of him or to write him off as unimportant. When he reappeared dangerously and decisively behind them, often in their penalty area, they had cause to regret it.

Too many soccer players think that to be effective they must be near to the ball, in possession of it or on the move all the time. There's little point in wanting the ball unless a player knows that he can use it better than any other player at that time. And there's little point in being on the move when it's a sheer waste of energy, quite apart from attracting the close attention of opponents.

Some animals know that to be still is to be unseen. Rabbits run: that's why they get shot !

It is unusual to see a mid-field player making long runs, for any reason other than to make a surprise entry into the opposing penalty area for a shot at goal. It's not so much the run but the timing of it and the line down which it is made which produces tactical problems. Both depend upon the player's ability to wait for the perfect opportunity.

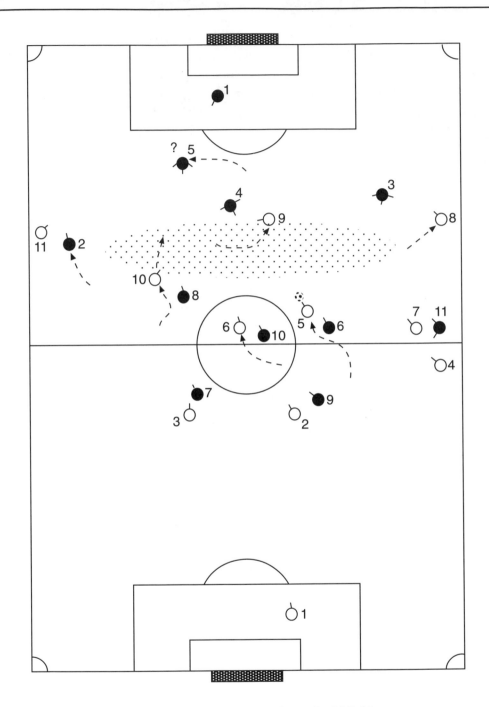

Diagram 55. In attack, midfielders must penetrate beyond mid-field opponents.

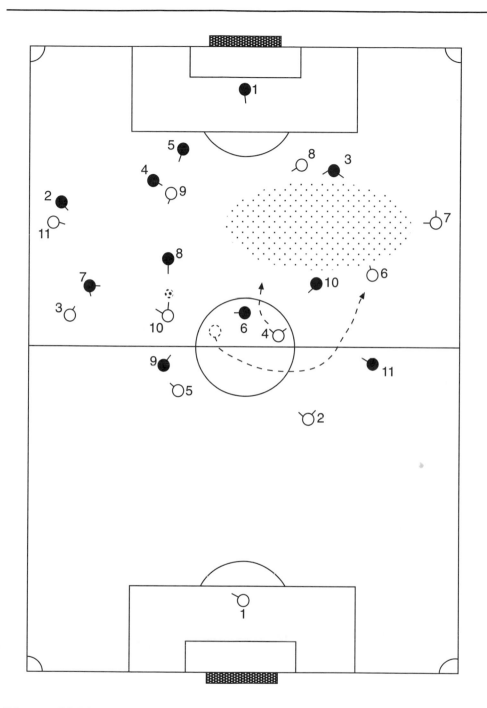

Diagram 56. Disappearing act: Where to reappear.

That will be when:
1. The flow of play is sideways, or diagonally forward and away from the mid-field player's starting position.
2. The sideways move triggers off what appears to be a positive and fairly direct counter attack.
3. The emergence of a threat draws the attention of the majority or all the defenders towards that side of the pitch.
4. The mid-field player delays his move until there is no chance of any opponent picking up his run when he is well on his way to the striking area.

The full-back furthest from the flank down which the counter attack is making ground will be best placed to pick up the mid-field player's run but if he does so he knows that the ball can be easily played fractionally longer to any wide attacker, white 7 in diagram 56, coming in from behind him. If the player with the ball can run it at the opposing defense he will attract all defensive attention for a time.

The further he goes, the greater the concern among the defenders about his intentions. The greater their concern about him, the less the attention paid to the vanishing act of the other mid-field player. This was the kind of run made to punishing effect, but not over frequently, by England captain and Manchester United mid-field star, Bryan Robson. Over-done and the move alerts defenders, even the confirmed ball watchers.

Finally, the success of such moves depends on the determination of the runner to get 'on the end' of any cross, come what may.

5.73 Effective Movement.

Attacking problems are most effectively set when opponents cannot be sure what the attackers' intentions are.

Players must study the reactions of opponents to different kinds of movement. As we have seen, quick movements by attackers alert defenders and provoke quick reactions from them. Sometimes, of course, attackers need to attract the attention of defenders and away from the intended moves of other more dangerous players. Quick obvious moves will achieve this, particularly if they are accompanied by confident, loud shouts for a pass.

The starting position for a dangerous attacking move is all important if advantages are to be maximized. Getting into that starting position is an important tactical skill.

In diagram 57, white 11 can see good counter attacking possibilities occurring on the far side of the pitch. The main obstacle to him getting into a shooting space. . . unmarked, is the full-back nearest to him. That full-back, being a good positional player, has already swung over into a covering position. The best tactical move for the mid-field player may be to walk towards a position wide of the full-back and almost in line with him. By walking, at best he may achieve his starting position undetected, at worst he is unlikely to worry the full-back unduly. . . especially if his walk is a disinterested stroll.

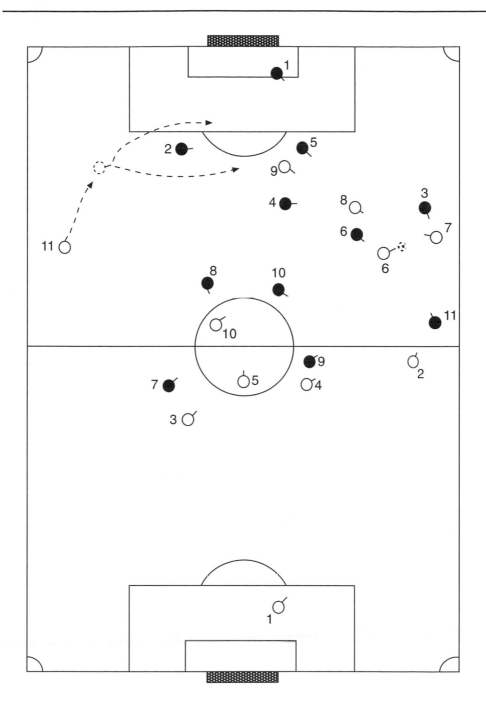

Diagram 57. Establishing dangerous positions by walking into them.

In either event, he has maneuvered himself into a starting position in which he is fifteen yards nearer to his target area than he was and in a semi blind-side position. When the moment to move arrives. . . the moment when it is clear that his team mate with the ball will be able to deliver it into the target area. . . he will cover the first five yards striding quietly and then accelerate into a full sprint. It is a certainty that he will gain several yards start on his opponent; a start which no opponent will make up.

5.74 Indirect Play.

In England, high jumping, powerful attackers have always been popular with coaches; their value has often been more imaginary than real. The aerial factor is regarded as a difficult option to counter: used cleverly and sparingly it is: used brainlessly and incessantly it certainly isn't. Some English coaches resorted to a strategy of all out aerial assault in the hope, presumably, that opponents would be intimidated by power and would crumple under the pressure. Defensive tactics in the advanced soccer nations solved those problems long ago.

Modern defenders, which often means every player in the team, are tactically aware enough to deal with direct aerial threats of that kind, in fact even the biggest attacker may be lucky to get off the ground against some of them. And they don't need big powerful defenders to do it! (see the volume in this series dealing with 'Back Play'). An aerial attack which can be direct or indirect is another matter however.

In his time one of the world's great strikers and one of three best attacking headers of a ball that I have ever seen, England's Tommy Lawton, was under six feet tall but could easily jump to head the ball downwards from a foot above the goal cross-bar. . . and if you think that's easy try it. But it wasn't so much the height and power which Lawton commanded, it was the heading control and accuracy with which he could drop the ball onto the foot (or the head) of another attacker.

Arriving late inside the penalty area, he timed his jumps so that he seemed to hang in the air while looking around and deciding where to play the ball. Ten yards from goal and he would head directly for it and score more often than not. Occasionally, however, he would head the ball away from goal to another attacker to shoot. It was this uncertainty about his intentions which caused opponents. . . even those who used illegal methods to try to stop him. . . so many problems.

The obvious and direct may be successful initially but eventually success will only be achieved when tactics include the indirect and the less obvious.

Indirect play involving interpassing moves. . . long and short: dribbling runs: slowing down the pace of play by varying the speed with which the ball is moved from player to player or from one area to another: altering the point of penetration . . . or threatening to: all are very important tactical considerations. Some have serious implications for the practice and improvement of certain techniques and all have implications for the attitudes of players.

All players must be educated to see and understand the purposes of direct and indirect playing tactics.

Carried to extremes, indirect play becomes negative and unproductive. Players become 'posers' and avoid responsibility for doing anything worthwhile. On the other hand totally direct play becomes crude and literally brainless. Players aren't required to make fine judgments or to act in any way imaginatively; they are programmed to react predictably and forcefully according to tactical pre-arrangements.

Unfortunately, as predictability fails, as it must, forceful play becomes violent and often dangerous.

Recently I watched a clever. . . and very quick. . . wide attacker in England trying, for most of ninety minutes, to beat his opponent. . . often two of them. . . on the outside.

He didn't! Clearly he hadn't the faintest idea of indirect play. Had he attacked his opponent on the inside a couple of times he would have found beating him on the outside that much easier. Superbly equipped as he was, because of his dribbling skills, to be an indirect player, he failed because he persisted in doing the expected . . . the direct. . . all the time.

5.75 Anticipation: Eliminating Opponents' Options.

Individual tactical skills in defense aim at keeping attackers 'off balance', tactically speaking, by continually anticipating. . . or seeming to anticipate. . . their intentions and by producing counter moves.

For example, a team may know that an attacker likely to oppose one of their wide backs is tricky, quick and difficult to contain when running at defenders. The team's agreed tactical objective might be to prevent the attacker receiving the ball by cutting off his supply. In the event of team tactics failing however, the wide back's personal tactics might be to prevent his opponent from receiving the ball when facing him or to prevent the attacker from turning with the ball should he actually get it. Success in either will effectively prevent the attacker from employing a technical or an athletic advantage.

The defender will need the freedom to position himself nearer to his opponent than he might against an opponent without those particular attributes. The defender's capacity for integrating his positional responsibilities, covering for example, with those of his co-defenders will be lessened.

Where a defender is faced by an attacker possessing outstanding technical or athletic abilities. . . or weaknesses. . . a defender will compel his opponent to choose action options which are least advantageous according to the circumstances. This may mean that team tactics have to be adapted to accommodate the personal tactical objectives of one player.

In the event, for example, of a mid-field player being faced with an opponent who is noticeably weak when moving to his left, that is to say onto his left foot, the mid-field defender must be allowed to 'jockey' his opponent onto that foot. Nearby defenders will adjust their marking and covering positions to take their team mate's personal tactical objective into account. These decisions often cannot be made before a match and require sympathetic understanding between players, sometimes to the temporary inconvenience of one or more players.

Soccer is, after all, a one for all and all for one game. Playing to make other players look better players is what team work is all about.

5.76 Threatening Moves.

I have referred to the need for players to become very sharp observers. Watching and remembering other players' movement mannerisms (body speak) is the most important first stage in anticipating what they are about to do. This applies just as much to the habits of team-mates as it does to opponents and for precisely the same reason. Clever defenders wait until they know that opponents are trying to read their defensive intentions and deliberately make moves. . . or pretend to make them. . . to create false impressions.

In diagram 58, knowing that a team is anxious to exploit the outstanding pace of a mid-field player, black 8, who favors attacking runs in support of his strikers. The opposing mid-field player, white 6, suspects that his opponents' intentions may be to play passes into the 'channels' wide of central defenders and behind himself. To make this option less attractive, white 6 waits until he sees an opponent 'ranging' such a pass (judging distance and target) and drops back five yards or so thereby giving himself a 'start' in any race for the ball into a wide channel. He makes the intended pass a much less attractive proposition and, having inhibited the pass he moves back into a much closer marking position.

Players who enjoy delivering long, accurate passes don't enjoy having their calculations upset.

Individual defenders may find themselves easily unbalanced and beaten by attackers with good dribbling control who are prepared to run the ball at them. In these circumstances it may pay defenders to run away from their opponents until the opponents slow down or until their control is less than perfect. It is almost certain that a speedy player with the ball, faced by an opponent running away from him WILL slow down. He slows down because the defender is stealing his ground and in effect gaining a start should there be a sprint for the ball played past the defender.

Most attackers like to tempt an opponent into tackling for the ball and so into an 'off balance' position, before making their decisive move past him: they tempt defenders into beating themselves. If a defender won't make such a move the attacker must.

Attackers with the ball must be made to take on the responsibility for making the first moves. The defender can afford to wait for his opponent to make the mistakes. Even so, the use of retreating tactics must be varied with feints to make what appear to be positive attempts to challenge for the ball. The attacker must be 'worked' and presented with changing defensive attitudes. Sometimes the defender will stand tall in front of the opponent but standing tall will be varied with a crouching and more aggressive looking posture. Sometimes the defender will move from an 'outside' to an 'inside' stance and back again, quickly. Retreating will be alternated with quick

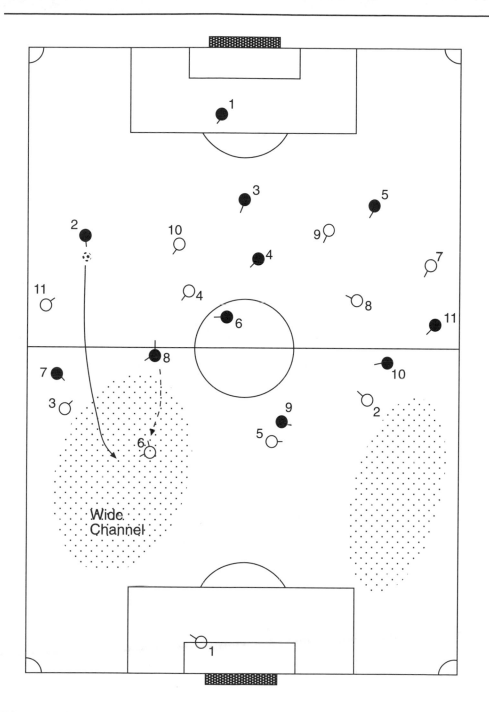

Diagram 58. Dropping off to threaten target space.

threats to move towards the attacker followed by equally quick moves away from him and so on. Outstanding defenders never allow opponents to do things in their own time. They never allow attackers to pose all questions; they work them into positions of having to find answers.

Truly great soccer players produce tactical and technical solutions to any problems but they pose so many problems for opponents that the opponents rarely have time to set any themselves. And there's an important clue in how to coach even difficult players. . . keep them working hard at solving problems for themselves. Kept busy, players haven't the time to cause problems for coaches!

Chapter 6
Advanced Techniques

A modern mid-field player needs the greatest possible range of techniques. The greater his technical range the greater the number of action options open to him. These increase the difficulties encountered by opponents trying to anticipate what his actions are likely to be.

The single greatest disadvantage for a mid-field player aiming to play top class soccer is having only one foot! If he can only use one foot effectively to control the ball or to pass it, he will find himself easily controlled by 'thinking' opponents. If he is only right footed, say, whenever he turns to his right to use his 'good' foot, he will find an opponent blocking his move. When, as he must, he turns onto his 'bad' foot he is immediately in deep trouble. Other opponents, well informed about his one foot handicap, close down on the passing options open to him. They know that he will be uncomfortable and less accurate (or useless) when forced onto his weak foot.

Although he may not know it, any player already skillful with one foot has enormous learning advantages over less skillful players. He has everything necessary to become a successful self-coach! If he thinks about it, he already knows how to perform the required skills. The techniques used for one foot are only mirror reflections of the same techniques on the other. His problem is to 'think transfer' what he does, from his good foot to the other. . . and it's not as difficult as it sounds.

Short, concentrated periods of thoughtful practice, no more than twenty minutes at a time, guarantee unbelievable results.

Some coaches think that the higher a player's status in the game, the more he should concentrate on practicing what he already does well. That is nonsense!

The returns gained from regular, thoughtful, short periods of practice of inadequate techniques, using his poorer foot, will pay huge dividends even in the short term. To be a one-footed player in high class soccer is to have the disadvantages, almost, of having a leg cut off.

Practice doesn't make perfect. . . but the right sort of practice does!

6.1 First Touch Skills: Passes, Volleys and Half Volleys.
The mid-field player, frequently under pressure, must be able to give passes instantly and precisely.
He must be able:
- (a) to assess and remember the positions and the movement of team mates and opponents. This gives him an ongoing perception of passing options,
- (b) to play the ball comfortably, in the air or on the ground.
- (c) to change the direction of the ball, into space or to a team mate using one or

at most two touches of the ball,

(d) to apply force or reduce force to the ball, as late as possible, as contact with it is made.

(e) to pass and move into another position thereby attracting one or more opponents into following him or offering himself for a subsequent pass.

Mid-field players must be able to move in one direction while passing in another, even opposite, direction. To do so he should master passing and controlling skills with all surfaces of both feet: instep, outside of the foot, inside of the foot and not least the heel. Using the inside of his foot a mature mid-field player will deliver volleyed, half volleyed or ground passes over distances up to twenty yards (on a wet top rather more) and with pin point accuracy.

6.11 Reversed Skills.

Probably the single most important aspect of learning (and teaching) soccer techniques is understood by few coaches and even fewer players and then only towards the ends of their careers.

All soccer techniques are perfectly reversible to produce exactly opposite effects.

For example, a short, volleyed pass is made using the inside of the foot swung, to strike the ball, on the end of a bent and firmly 'held' knee. The foot is swung along an imaginary line through the ball towards the target. Alternatively, when preparing to volley a pass, the player may play the pass with a loose knee and ankle and with little follow through: he absorbs much of the ball's force to control and shorten the pass.

If, having commenced the forward leg swing to pass, he reverses the movement, fractionally before the ball makes contact with his foot, all its force will be lost and the ball will drop at his feet. All 'striking' techniques using any part of the body, if reversed, produce an opposite effect to the pass: they produce a 'stopping effect' and the ball is dropped at the player's feet.

Most young players will benefit from learning each passing technique and its reverse or controlling technique at the same time.

Having a second action option, instantly changeable by skillful players, is the way to the top. Faced by such a player who can, with no obvious change in action, control the ball or pass it, opponents are never absolutely certain what he will do.

Usually they wait to see; that is how skillful players gain time.

All actions leading up to an 'either or' skill must always be the same, giving no clue as to a player's real intentions. It is also important that the player learns to give the pass (or to control the ball) with all the different surfaces of his feet; the inside, the instep (the top of the foot), the outside and even with the sole of the foot.

High skill is shown when a player can make deceptive passes with his or her heel.

6.12 Half-volley Techniques.

These are a must for playing in any class of soccer in which, occasionally, players must play with one touch only. This is particularly so when a player receives an aerial pass and needs to deliver a ground pass with time for no more than one touch to do so. The second receiver may be in a shooting position but closely marked and therefore needs to shoot instantly. He is likely to make more of a pass along the ground than one in the air.

In high class soccer taking more than one touch to achieve optimum control or effect may be one touch too many.

Played most skillfully, soccer is played on the ground. Aerial passes are needed only when ground passing options are not available. High class players accept the challenge of giving perfectly weighted and absolutely accurate ground passes, even through the narrowest of gaps. They pass for the benefit of the receiver. Poor players give any sort of pass; they pass for their own benefit.

The true test of quality in a soccer player is his success in making the game as easy as possible for his team mates. He tries to foresee all the problems which receiving players are likely to have and eliminate them.

Key factors in delivering half volley passes are:
  (a) 'Faking' a volley; this checks the challenge of an opponent. The receiver gains time to take a pace backwards and allow the ball to drop to the ground.
  (b) 'Seeing' a line through the ball to the target, at the exact spot at which it will hit the ground.
  (c) Calculating accurately the space through which the pass must travel.
  (d) Never caught (seen) making the above judgments.

If a player can't make accurate assessments with one look, in good class soccer he may struggle. Any further assessment will give the game away to opponents. . . at least it will to the wide-awake ones!

  (e) Accelerating the foot smoothly through the ball's horizontal mid-line. . . or slightly above it. . . just as the ball hits the ground. Half volleys are swept towards the target rather than hit.
  (f) Transferring weight through the ball at impact and on line to the target.

All passing (kicking) techniques should result in a slight overbalance towards the passer's target after the ball has left his foot.

6.2 Ground and Aerial Drives.

Effective mid-field players must have the perception to 'range' their passing options (judge height, distance and power needs) accurately and quickly. In 'pro' soccer they have little time in which to judge angles, movement and distances and even less to deliver the ball. They must be able to change kicking actions, very late. A ground drive to a player twenty to thirty yards away may have to be changed to a steeply angled 'chip' (a nine iron shot to golfers) over one or more opponents hit with back spin to hold the ball close to the target. Even a lofted drive, covering fifty yards, to a player running at full speed, may be the power change required.

There are two key factors in hiding a change in kicking action needed to produce differing results.

    (a) The length of the kicking leg from hip to toe as the foot strikes the ball. A bent knee in effect shortens the leg and reduces the power delivered; a stretched leg increases power and, at the right angle, distance.

    (b) Where the foot strikes the ball in relation to the horizontal mid-line through it.

Given the same swing, in length of leg and speed of foot, the further the contact point is below the mid-line, the higher the angle of flight. A contact point half way between the horizontal mid-line and the ground gives a flight angle of about 45 degrees and optimum distance.

A ball hit as low as possible, below the ball's point of contact with the ground, will create optimum lift and back spin. The ball's trajectory will be short and steep.

Frequent reference has been made to the need to hide intentions when passing the ball, long or short. It is by studying all players' kicking actions carefully that good professionals can tell, often on the minutest of action changes, just what an opponent's intentions are. For that reason, players wishing to become outstanding mid-field distributors of the ball must practice to delay any change in kicking action as late as possible before contact with the ball is made.

6.21 Spin and Swerve.

A ball has two mid-lines, one vertical and one horizontal. If the ball is kicked to one side or the other of the vertical mid-line the ball will spin sideways. Kicked below the horizontal mid-line the ball will spin backwards and kicked above it the ball travels with forward spin or roll. Kicked below the horizontal mid-line and to one side of the vertical mid-line the ball spins, lifts and swerves.

In still air, swerve is produced by sideways spin on the ball: lift by back spin. The greater the speed of ball spin the greater the swerve or lift effect.

The Chip.
Optimum height over the shortest distance is achieved:

- when the ball is struck at its lowest point in relation to the ground: ___ effectively beneath it.
- the faster the foot speed at contact, the greater the back spin and the higher the lift.

The following general rules affect spin and swerve irrespective of the intended direction and effect.

Principles.
(a) The larger the area of the striking surface, the more controlled and predictable the spin and swerve will be.

(b) The smaller the striking area, the toe for example, the more the ball shape is distorted by the kick and the less predictable its flight. Elasticity causes the ball to change shape rapidly as it fights to regain its original shape.

(c) The longer the contact between foot and ball, the greater its effect on distance, flight and ball movement.

(d) The further the contact point is from the ball's centre, the less the forward flight and the greater the spin .

Contact eventually becomes so 'thin', i.e. near to the ball's outer surface, as to cause the ball to spin almost without moving in any direction.

The inflated pressure in the ball, i.e. its hardness, has an important effect. The softer the ball the more unpredictable the flight. It is in the interests of goalkeepers to ask for soccer balls to be inflated to the highest allowed pressure. . . even harder if they can get away with it!

A ball traveling through air is subject to similar effects as the air (e.g. the wind) traveling past a ball. An opposing wind builds up air pressure against the ball. Ball spin has a similar effect. Air pressure in both cases resists the flight of the ball and directs it along less resistant paths. The ball swerves or lifts or even swerves and lifts.

Soccer balls facing resistance, e.g. air pressure, move in the direction of least resistance. That is why swerve follows the direction of spin. Wind, of course, produces a much stronger resistance to the ball's flight hence deflection is increased. Good players use the wind to increase deception in their passes.

Receiving players must be able to 'allow' for the ball continuing to move. . . to swerve or spin. . . while they are trying to control or pass it.

6.22 Drag.
A ground drive can be swerved round an opponent but only over a relatively short distance. A great deal of kicking power has to be used to gain a relatively small swerve effect; spin being resisted by the ground itself. The thicker and the drier the grass the greater the resistance: the shorter and the wetter the grass the less the

resistance. Both will cause the ball to skid for part of its travel with no spin at all. This is known as the 'drag' effect.

The ball is struck through a point some way below the mid line but with a vertical kicking surface (the instep). The toe is allowed to slide underneath the ball as it begins its forward travel. The back spin imparted is countered by the forward momentum of the ball. The ball neither rolls nor spins backwards, it skids in the direction of the pass until forward speed overcomes the backspin.

Drag reduces the range of a pass but can be used by skillful players to deceive opponents. A pass hit with 'drag' has to be struck with more force than the range of the pass justifies. Opponents deceived by the power put into the pass may think interception impossible. In fact actual ball speed is much less than it seems because the drag effect is working against the ball's line of travel.

'Drag' is particularly useful for passing through the narrowest of gaps between opponents, over relatively short distances, on pitches which are wet and where the grass is quite long. Additionally, drag makes a pass more easily controlled by pass receivers.

Players who seek to become 'master' players must experiment with and master these and other advanced techniques.

6.23 'Effortless' Passing.

It is impossible to pass the ball over distances in excess of forty yards without considerable effort but the hallmark of pass perfection is the ability to seem to do so. The principles governing pass control and distance we have studied earlier.

The key is in the reduction of the length of the back swing of the kicking leg. A player must develop optimum foot acceleration speed from a much shorter than normal back lift. Reducing the back lift deceives opponents into thinking that the range of the pass is going to be shorter than it is. A slow initial leg swing with final acceleration as late as possible confirms that deception. This ability to develop late power is a matter of increasing the speed and strength of contraction in those muscles which begin and carry the kicking action through. It is also a matter of developing 'timing': generating the right speed at exactly the right time. That's what practice is all about.

6.3 Instant Control.

Time, in soccer, is limited by a player's capacity for working out his options early.

Having chosen an action option, time is governed by the speed with which he can bring the right skill into use. The less time he takes the more time he makes. . . for his team mates. Players who take their time do it at the expense of their team mates. They are time thieves. Players who are slow thinkers are slow 'doers' and slow 'doers' are 'obvious' players; unfortunately they are as obvious to opponents as they are to team mates.

Instant control, with any part of the body. . . except hands or arms. . . leaving opponents with no chance of stealing the ball , gives a player time. A player with time not only controls WHAT will happen, he controls WHEN it will happen.

In first class soccer any player not certain of bringing any pass under immediate control. . . in the air, on the ground, in playing conditions varying between rock hard and swamp soft, in high wind or driving rain. . . causes endless problems. . . for everyone. Too many players lacking sureness in control get themselves out of trouble by passing first touch. . . to 'anyone'. Usually 'anyone' is landed in more trouble than the player who made the pass.

Passing the ball too soon and carelessly is as selfish as hanging onto it too long.

The following factors are crucial in controlling, instantly, even the hardest hit pass.
   (a) The intended controlling surface must be relaxed and softened.
   (b) The controlling surface is drawn away from the ball's line of travel fractionally before the ball hits that surface.

Even when both ball and player are in mid air the same principles apply and control effectiveness will be just as great as if the player was on the ground.

A relaxed (soft) controlling surface being withdrawn absorbs the force of the ball and the ball 'dies' at the player's feet. This is known in the game as 'killing' the ball.

In the 1978 World Cup final I counted in excess of forty free kicks awarded before half time and the number should have been sixty. Most were given for intimidation or for 'accidentally' colliding with opponents as or just after they attempted to control the ball.

Skillful players must be protected from foul play and from intimidation. The alternative is generations of 'pin-ball' players: players who have no intention of bringing the ball under control: players who get rid of the ball before it arrives almost. Some countries already have them and wonder why.

Mid-field players, under constant pressure from opponents, must be able to accept the ball on any part of the body and drop it at their feet and they must be protected from illegal interference while doing so.

6.31 Controlling and Screening.

Having controlled the ball but under immediate challenge, players must be able to turn while using their body to screen (hide) the ball from an opponent. Having controlled and screened the ball, the player can position himself to pass or to dribble past opponents.

Mid-field players, always in the thick of the action, need this ability to receive, control and to hide the ball more than most.

Screening the ball while dribbling demands very close control of the ball and to achieve it, the ball is directed using frequent touches to move it only relatively short distances. The ball is kept within a few inches of the dribbling player's foot enabling him to change direction or to stop and start, quickly and easily.

6.32 Controlling and Turning.

Advanced controlling techniques require players to control the ball and turn in the same movement often with only one touch. Top class opponents are so quick to intercept, to tackle or to take up a skin-tight marking position that opposing mid-field players must master limited touch techniques.

Success in one-touch controlling and turning is based first on deception. The player seeking to turn with the ball must persuade opponents that he will not control the ball but pass it, perhaps first touch.

Remember, 'reverse' skills enable a player to reverse any action to produce an exactly opposite effect.

All the player's movements will 'sell' an impression that he intends to pass the ball but at the last second, he reverses a towards-the-ball passing movement into an away-from-the-ball controlling movement. The fake pass will cause the opponent to hold-off. Opponents only go through with challenges when convinced that they can gain possession of the ball, legally or illegally.

To turn and control the ball at chest height or higher, the receiver will feint to head the ball, changing (reversing) the heading action into chest control with a turn in the last split second. The player must give himself that extra second in which to reverse his action by developing a totally convincing fake move.

Movement mannerisms when faking to pass, kick or head must be identical with those which precede actual passing, kicking or heading moves. Many players use head and eye movements to deceive opponents, especially tight markers. If the mid-field player lifts his head sharply to look over his right shoulder as he receives the ball. He creates the impression that he may move or play the ball in that direction. His marker may react by following his head movement. The mid-field player reverses and spins off to his left and away from his opponent.

Looking. . . and often calling. . . in one direction, as if to move or to play there, and then spinning away in the other, is a trick which works even against quality players.

A receiving player may seem to assume a half turned position some way before the ball arrives and before his opponent needs to challenge. In fact he is telegraphing his intentions to invite his opponent to try for an interception. As the ball arrives he will speed up one stride towards it before allowing the ball to pass his front foot. As the ball contacts his rear foot, he turns that foot inwards and deflects the ball behind his front foot enabling to him to turn in the same direction and away from the challenge.

6.4 Running the Ball and Dribbling.

Running with the ball is not the same skill as dribbling. Both, of course, require a player to be able to run with the ball at varying speeds while maintaining enough control to stop the run and restart it as circumstances demand.

Dribbling, however, usually means that an attacker with the ball deliberately seeks to confront a defender. He does this by taking the ball towards the opponent or by drawing the opponent towards the ball. Dribbling then involves a wide variety of manipulative tricks and feints to deceive the opponent and to move past him. These tricks are used to draw the opponent off balance at which time he is in no position to prevent the attacker moving past him.

Running with the ball, on the other hand, involves the simple skill of moving the ball directly and usually urgently from one area to another. Ball runners, more often than not, try to avoid confrontation with opponents but if necessary, opponents are beaten more by change of pace and direction, allied to power, than by sheer cleverness.

It isn't vital that a mid-field player has the trickery and the manipulative skills of a high class dribbler. He will have other abilities which are more important. . . a tactical brain, instant control and wide passing vision, power and skill in taking advantage of shooting positions and so on. It IS vital that he develops the ability and the determination to run the ball positively and very strongly when the occasion demands it.

6.41 Changing Acceleration.

The greater the number of players committed to the struggle for mid-field control, the less the space available for successful interpassing moves. To break up this log jam, players who are prepared to hold the ball by screening (shielding) it from opponents while running it powerfully away from congested areas and where possible at back defenders, are invaluable. Running the ball is the only sensible alternative to passing in these circumstances. Carried out suddenly and with determination, it introduces the element of surprise upon which successful soccer depends.

The primary surprise element in running the ball, when followed or challenged by an opponent, is the ability to accelerate from slow to fast, or from fast to very fast, smoothly (effortlessly): that is to say with little if any perceptible change in running action. Most players who develop this skill do so first by learning to run with the ball using a comfortable, relaxed stride. This is rather less than the stride length used when sprinting all out. They learn how to lengthen their stride by increasing their relaxation even more while doing so: at the same time maintaining or slightly increasing their stride pattern. Stride pattern, or cadence as it is called in track athletics, is the number of times the feet hit the ground during a run over any given distance. Clearly, if his stride is lengthened slightly a player will cover any given distance quicker than he would using a shorter stride. Similarly if he keeps his stride length the same and increases (speeds up) his stride pattern (cadence), he will also cover that distance quicker. If he increases stride length and cadence at the same time, he will cover the same distance more quickly still.

Deception, when running the ball, is in the player's ability to appear more relaxed the faster he runs. Too often, players trying to run extra fast feel a need to make all the body work harder: tension increases even in those parts of the body which contribute nothing to the running action. In these circumstances, the limited amount of fuel which the body can make available for hard work of any kind is not concentrated where it should be, in those parts of the body which cause a player to run faster or longer.

This makes running hard work and, even worse in soccer, it shows opponents that the player IS working hard which alerts them to the need to work hard themselves. Running fast, in soccer, is achieved through the hips and everything below them. The arms and upper body are used for soccer balance which is quite different from sprinting balance. Soccer balance is used to control a ball AND to prepare the runner for instant employment of a soccer skill. A fifty metre sprint race between Olympic champion Carl Lewis and Argentina's world soccer star Maradonna would be a walk-over for Maradonna. . . if both had to sprint with a soccer ball at their feet.

The secret of deceptive acceleration is in the ability to relax and to SEEM to be capable of stopping and starting, changing pace and changing direction effortlessly. And the right sort of practice WILL lead to perfection.

One final point, an attacker running the ball is infinitely more difficult to deal with if he can accelerate, stop and start and change direction using either foot to do so. An attacker able to move off only one foot and therefore in only one direction is easy meat for the thinking defender. . . and thinking defenders ARE on the increase!

6.42 Stopping and Starting and Feint Plays Over The Ball.

A player with the ball controls the timing of any action by him or against him. Opponents must react to what he does and they will always be fractionally behind him at the start. A player who can stop and start suddenly has an important initial advantage over an opponent. In athletic terms he himself fires the gun which starts the race. The exception will be when an opponent out guesses him or 'reads' the attacker's movement mannerisms which warn him what the attacker is likely to do.

Deceptive stopping, by a player running the ball, is best achieved when he pretends to accelerate before stopping. The nearer he is to goal, the greater the need for a defender to cover the attacker's run but all defending players, to a degree, take any attempt to run the ball past them as a personal affront. Consequently they may be over inclined to counter that threat as early as possible. . . sometimes too early. This enables the attacker's 'stop' to be that much more effective, hence the fake move to sprint before stopping. Similarly any intention to accelerate away with the ball should be preceded by an action indicating that the player is about to stop or to actually do so.

A player half turns his body to allow him to place his leading foot in front of the ball, as if to stop it. The rear foot is the foot which will play the ball forward should he decide to accelerate away rather than stop. Some players become very skillful at running the ball at speed while frequently producing these fake stop and start movements.

It is easy to make a very late decision on whether to stop or not using this technique. Similarly a player may pass one foot over the ball momentarily as if to stop it with the sole of his foot. The move may be real or fake and is changed from one to the other merely by lifting or lowering the foot. Any move to place one foot in front of the ball, or on top of it, while running at speed will be seen, by an opponent, as a warning that the ball runner may be about to stop. Any foot movement towards the back of the ball will be seen as an intention to begin to run or to continue running with it. In either case, any foot move towards the ball, apparently to stop or to start, can be changed into a fake movement to the side of or over the ball.

Mid-field players must learn these 'fake' skills. The more realistically they are used, the greater the capability of the mid-field player for breaking up soccer's mid-field log jam and making space for himself and others. Dribbling players often develop exaggerated versions of these fake moves. They do so to goad opponents into impatient even angry challenges.

Ball runners, because their movements are more urgent and threatening, need only the slightest of fake moves to throw opponents out of stride. The runner's speed and therefore the speed of his feint move at the ball means that an opponent has to react much more quickly than he would wish. Rather than be caught flat footed and left behind, defenders are inclined to 'buy' fake moves and become that much more vulnerable.

6.43 Hiding or Showing The Ball.

A player running the ball while controlling it with the foot furthest from a tracking defender is difficult to dispossess without fouling him.

As the attacker varies his pace and makes fake moves to stop and start, the ball will be hidden (screened) from the defender. He may be tempted into tackling across the attacker which, if the attacker hides the ball skillfully, will be hopeful rather than certain. Careless tackles near to or in the penalty area are severely punished.

A player screening the ball must learn to run with the ball at speed while splitting his attention between controlling the ball on one side in relation to the position, movements and intentions of his opponent on the other; keeping an opponent on his blind side is important in tempting and evading a tackle.

An attacker running the ball with his inside foot, the foot nearer to an opponent, is tantamount to 'showing' him the ball. Showing an opponent the ball is to tempt him into tackling for it. The attacker must be absolutely sure of his speed and control in being able to play the ball away from the tackle before the opponent contacts it.

Both hiding and showing the ball while running it have advantages and disadvantages. Running the ball while hiding it inside the penalty area can earn penalties from ill judged sliding tackles. . and they ARE made!

Running the ball with the inside foot and showing an opponent the ball tempts an opponent to tackle when the advantage of moving clear of the tackle should be with the attacker. That is why it can be a major advantage for a wide player on the right to be able to run the ball. . . or to dribble it. . . with his left or inside foot. As he pulls the ball outside the tackling player the attacker moves naturally into his running stride. The problem occurs if, having beaten his opponent and gained a crossing position, he can't cross the ball using his outside foot. To check back and inside onto his favored foot gives a recovering opponent a second chance to tackle or to block the cross.

A one-footed, wide attacker who cannot deliver crosses accurately on the run with his outside foot is seriously flawed as a player at the top levels of soccer. As I have already said, the development of two footed skills cannot be over emphasized for all serious soccer players.

6.44 Body Swerve.

Over the years a number of great soccer players have shown an amazing ability to lean the body one way while moving the other and all done in the blink of an eye . . . apparently! And the operative word when describing body swerve IS 'apparently.'

Players wanting to move to the right, say, while running the ball at speed, will lean slightly towards their intended direction. The faster they are running the more obvious the lean. As we have already discussed, fast movements by a player with the ball cause fast. . . or faster. . . responses from opponents. If, while running the ball at speed. . . directly at an opponent. . . a player can produce a quick leaning movement without actually changing direction, opponents are likely to 'read' the lean as the intention to move in that direction. The attacker leans and regains his balanced running position all in one smooth movement. The action is so quick that a spectator receives the impression that the attacker has swerved round his opponent when, usually, the opponent has been moved fractionally out of the attacker's path or at least 'frozen'.

In modern professional soccer, body swerve almost disappeared from the game when defenders were allowed to use the dangerous and illegal skill of 'body checking'. Body checking among heavily protected ice hockey players is one thing, against unprotected soccer players it led to career terminating injuries.

A fast ball runner needs only the smallest swerve (lean) to throw his opponent off balance. The secret is in the timing of the dummy move; too soon and the opponent will refuse to 'buy' it; too late and the opponent will not have time to buy it!

Having developed momentum by running the ball into space, a player who changes his run suddenly, directly at a defender is likely to find that the defender 'freezes'. Defenders unused to opponents running towards them at speed haven't time to readjust their thinking and they are likely to be caught standing still.

In these circumstances, the attacking player looks for 'wall passing' assistance to one side of the defender, or he tries to send the defender the wrong way. The attacker uses his body swerve to play the ball past the defender on one side, while the attacker sways past him on the other. Most defenders, in this situation, crouch and spread their feet to enable them to take off to sprint with the attacker in any direction. Rather than play the ball past the defender, the attacker may find it possible to play the ball through the defender's legs. In English soccer this technique is called 'nutmegging' an opponent. . . but don't ask me why! The success of these and similar moves lies in an attacker's ability to 'sell a dummy' at speed; that is to say use a slight body and arm or head and eye movement to create the impression that the attacker will do one thing when he intends to do just the opposite. The higher a player intends to go in the game, the more important the ability to invent 'fake' moves becomes.

A dribbling player may use more exaggerated 'dummies' to deceive his opponent. He must be careful that the lean of his body swerve isn't so pronounced that he has difficulty regaining the balanced position needed to enable him to move away in the opposite direction. Stanley Matthews, England's 'wizard of dribble' always moved the ball towards his opponent using the most delicate of touches from the inside of each foot alternately to do so. This forward movement tended to cause a defender to back away and therefore to have his weight over his heels. When Matthews detected that his opponent had made up his mind not to retreat any further, he swayed to his left as if to move inside his opponent and immediately swerved right and outside him; always to his left and always outside his opponent! Sounds easy doesn't it? It certainly looked it. My own son, at fourteen years of age, could present a superb imitation of what Stanley Matthews did; everyone in England, including all his opponents, knew what he did: unfortunately they didn't know WHEN he was going to do it! Matthews's success was the result first, of enormous patience in 'working' his opponent into the required position and, even more importantly, into the right frame of mind. . . worried (!); second, his superb ability to 'read' the balance and the imbalance of a defender and, finally, his acute perception of precisely how much body swerve was needed to 'move' the opponent one way and make him vulnerable to Matthews's outside break. I have seen no more than two or three players throughout the world who possessed this ability to mesmerize opponents. The great Brazilian winger Garrincha, undoubtedly had it and so did Northern Ireland's genius of a player, George Best.

The skill of dribbling depends upon two different ball running techniques. The first, the Scottish method, involves keeping the ball under very close control by playing the ball forward using frequent light taps at the ball and very short running steps to do so. The ball is kept as close to the dribbling foot as possible and the body is 'hunched' over the ball. This head down position gives the impression that the player's attention is concentrated on the ball and that he has only a restricted awareness. . . if any. . . of what is happening in the vicinity of his dribbling run. The dribbling player gives the impression that he can't do anything else other than dribble because his head is always down. English pros claim that Scottish dribblers only play against legs because that's all that they ever see. In fact poor dribblers CAN'T do anything else but dribble and their heads ARE always down!.

Clever dribblers, of course. . . Scottish or otherwise. . . can dribble or pass as the occasion demands because their heads are up. This dribbling technique means that the ball is played in front of the body: the dribbler is much more erect with his head held high enabling him to see all playing options. The ball is 'held' on the bottom edge of his vision which allows him to exercise closer control when tackles are imminent.

Outstanding dribblers often allow the ball to move to what seems to be the extreme front limit of a reasonable controlling stride, thereby giving opponents the impression that the ball isn't really under control and drawing them into a tackle. A split second before the tackle arrives, the player lengthens his stride to flick the ball away and accelerate after it.

6.5 Heading.

The techniques of heading for mid-field players are not all that different from those used by other players but the conditions in which they have to head the ball differ enormously. Consequently mid-field players need specific practice aimed at reproducing those conditions.

6.51 Aerial Heading.

Player-to-player pressure is greater in mid-field than in any other phase of play, corner kicks and free kicks near to the penalty area excepted. Consequently the ball may be in the air unexpectedly and often. . . at least in England it is! This means that mid-field players have to jump to head when they have had little if any time to prepare to take off. And that's difficult.

Even the slightest pre-jump movement of the feet, of one foot or of the arms and body will help a player to gain more height than he will without a preparatory move. Any movement to overcome complete inertia is valuable.

If possible, the player should jump to head (nod) the ball downwards to a team mate's feet, heading it upwards usually means anywhere, to an opponent or to a team mate. In any case, if heading downwards in this phase of play is accepted by the whole team as a tactical aim, all players will be prepared for it.

If, when taking off, a player can turn his body in the air before reaching heading height, he may find that the turn of his upper body has the effect of moving any close jumping opponent off-line and unable to contact the ball easily.

Jumping to head the ball for a mid-field player unable to gain the height he would expect from a run and jump, will require him to develop a 'flick' heading technique. Contact with the ball is made by that part of the forehead where the front meets the side and the head is flicked sideways at the ball. The flick is timed to coincide with the peak of the player's jump.

6.52 Heading 'Off' The Ground.

If the ball runs free and bounces, any player running to meet the ball must be prepared to knock the ball on with his head even when running at top speed. Whether he has to run and jump to contact the ball or bend forward to head it while running, he uses the flat front of his forehead to guide the ball forward so that it falls and 'dies' at the player's feet and 'in stride'. He should be able to bring the ball under control, to pass, shoot or dribble on, with one touch only.

A mid-field player has a need for heading skills which emphasize short distance accuracy and sensitivity of touch rather than distance or power. Having said that, a tall or high jumping mid-field player able to head with power and distance has a considerable advantage over players lacking these capabilities. They allow him to dominate mid-field aerial battles, particularly those where the ball is delivered towards him from his opponents' defensive positions, by heading the ball down and back towards the feet of his own strikers.

Opposing defenders are most vulnerable to counter attack when they have just cleared the ball from danger areas. . or think they have!

To be a major influence in all aspects of play, a mid-field player needs the widest possible range of skills at the highest possible levels. He plays in pressure situations most of the time and his 'touch' and perception have to be finely tuned. Here I have specified special techniques which he should master; they should give him a competitive edge. He must be able to shoot and to get into the most profitable shooting positions. He must be able to mark, intercept, cover and tackle as well as any defender.

The work rate required of a great mid-fielder will be exceptional and his athletic and gymnastic preparation, from a very early age. . . seven or eight years . . . must reflect anticipated demands. Above all he must be difficult for opponents to 'pin down' and this quality, given all the other skills referred to, depends upon his ability to be two footed. If he practices so that he can use either foot with equal facility he is worth two players who can play with only the one foot.

The sooner he begins to think and practice as a double footed player, the better!

Chapter 7
Practice and Training

Most of the great players within my experience have found ways to practice alone, with one friend or within a small group through which, if they can't create realistic soccer situations, they can create exciting, imaginary ones. Great players become great because they develop an obsessive love for soccer and its skills and because they IMAGINE THEMSELVES TO BE IN ACTUAL SOCCER SITUATIONS whenever they are playing with a ball. Even when practicing by themselves, with a ball against a fence or a wall, they SEE themselves and what they are doing in the context of a major match or in a World Cup final. This ability to create a world of fantasy in which even elementary, 'singles' practices come alive is a very important condition in the early development of young soccer players. I suspect that it is exactly the same for young players in any sport. Young basketball players scrimmaging one on one under a single, back-street backboard see themselves as great players playing at the very highest levels of the game. Six and seven year old ice hockey players, working out on a frozen pond in Canada or Russia practice and play. . . which at that age is the same thing. . . with and against the game's greatest players, in their imaginations.

Without imagination practice becomes drudgery and drudgery never inspired anyone to be anything.

That lesson should be imprinted on the minds of every aspiring coach in any sport. Unimaginative, poorly trained coaches impose rigid, soul destroying, training regimes upon players which kill the love of play and practice which players must once have had to reach high skill levels. From sheer pleasure, soccer practice becomes painful and boring: the players become disillusioned.

The only true measure of practice effectiveness is in the change (improvement) which practice brings about in a player's performance in the game.

Performance change takes different forms. Individual techniques may need changing. e.g. a mid-fielder's use of his 'bad' foot, under pressure when defending in dangerous areas say, may be unacceptably risky. Practice designed to bring about a much increased inclination to use it in match play may be relatively simple: 'child's play' in fact with no more than two, maybe three players involved.

On the other hand the interpassing and support play skills between three mid-field players may have become tentative and unreliable. Practice aimed at re-establishing mutual confidence in different game situations, when, where and how to move forward in support of attacking play for example, will be more complex and involve more players. A number of practice considerations are implied: a wider range of passing techniques: a better appreciation of positional relationships; widened perceptions of forward passing and forward moving possibilities and fluid but safe positional interchanges.

A final last example might be focused on the need for improved containment and deflection of opposing attacking play, where opposing mid-field and back players are breaching the mid-field, first defensive curtain too easily. Practice implications here are very complex since they are likely to involve seven or eight players and a similar number of opponents at different stages in practice progression.

At the risk of being repetitive, the key factor in ensuring that practice is effective is realism.

Practice situations MUST be as close as possible to the match-play situations for which change (improvement) is sought.

For single techniques, e.g. long passing with the left foot only, or for technique 'groups', e.g. long passing into space behind opponents for forward moving attackers in its entirety, players may practice effectively in twos or threes if they are highly motivated towards improvement and if they have the capacity for imagining that they are actually playing in real matches while they are practicing.

As the number of assisting players increases, the greater the need, and the sooner the need, for the involvement of players to oppose the practice. Decision making skills in soccer are developed most effectively when players practice together and against opponents. The skill of controlling, limiting or increasing opposition while ensuring practice success and progress is the hall mark of a soccer coach of the highest class. Opposition in practice will usually be controlled, even limited, in the extent to which it is applied. Practice must be focused fairly precisely and the 'patients', much more often than not, must be successful.

Some 'coaches' are excellent producers of entertaining, even amusing practice programs: everyone enjoys their sessions, not too much thinking (if any) and a lot of laughs. These coaches are entertaining and amusing only while the team is doing well: when it isn't, the players need a much more perceptive and realistic approach to their problems.

In some countries desk-bound, wheeling and dealing managers backed up, more often than not, by ill equipped 'physical' trainers or entertainment 'directors', have had a disastrous effect upon styles of play and skill levels in the game.

Anyone with insight into modern player preparation visiting an English 'pro' club during training is likely to see the players playing six, seven or eight a side games or running, often reluctantly. The manager coach will be an active, sometimes noisy participant in the first but not in the second: definitely not! The running will be haphazard, unplanned, lapping of the stadium and based upon physiological principles best known to the 'motivator' but unrecognizable by any modern athletics coach. There will be little if any thoughtfully structured, progressive practice and no individual practice worth talking about.

7.1 Players' Needs.

Practice and training examples given here are drawn from the 'needs' indicated by analysis of match situations; I call them related practices. Individual or small group practices, to be effective, demand high levels of player motivation. That means that players must be educated to motivate themselves or they must be under the motivational supervision of a coach. . . more likely a mixture of both. In more complex practices, involving opposition to the practicing players, the complexity of the practice itself invokes a high degree of realism. Nevertheless the self motivation and coach motivation referred to earlier are still vitally important.

Quite simply, players at all levels must:
a) UNDERSTAND and ACCEPT the need for practice.
b) UNDERSTAND exactly HOW a practice is designed to help them and how it will work.
c) KNOW BY WHAT criteria they or the coach will judge the change in performance achieved.
d) SUSTAIN a high level of SELF MOTIVATION for the practice period.
e) KNOW THE RESULT OF PRACTICE immediately after each practice run.
f) AGREE HOW practice will be readapted to meet changing needs as a result of (d) previously.

7.2 'Singles' practice.

There is a belief in senior soccer that players will not practice in ways similar to those used when they were young. Individual rebound practice against a wall, for example, is seen by 'sophisticated' coaches as childish. Child 'based' it may be, but if that was how young players, uncoached often, learned the touch and the technical skill needed to become great players, it will do for me and for most of the players in my experience.

Personal practice IS best carried out against a rebound surface of some kind, a wall or a rebound board. An angle formed where two walls join adds possibilities and a practice space ten yards or more in width between two walls will be invaluable. A perfectly flat surface is not important for the same reason that a perfect ground practice surface isn't. Players who develop their skills on rough, bumpy practice surfaces are better able to cope with unpredictable playing pitches throughout their playing lives.

7.21 Volleys and Half Volleys.

Make marks on the wall at 3' and 5' in height. Make a mark on the ground parallel with the wall and 5 yards from it. Standing behind the ground mark, play successive volleys above the 5' mark.

Rebounding off the wall, the ball's first bounce must be behind the ground mark. In early stages, a player may allow the ball to bounce a maximum of three times before he plays it back to the wall. As he improves, he will reduce the ground bounce to one.

Progression 1.

As previously but playing the ball alternately above the 3' and then above the 5' wall marks.

One bounce only behind the ground mark.

Progression 2.
As previously using the 'other' (weaker) foot.

Progression 3.
Having drawn two marks down the wall, 2' apart and parallel to each other, repeat the previous progression using the outside of the feet to hit the ball against the wall wide of the two vertical marks, so that spin brings the ball back to the player's central position.

Progression 4.
Using a wall 'angle' and similar markings to those used on the single wall, play the volleys off each wall onto the next and return the ball back to feet.

'Singles' practices against a wall need practice targets i.e. a set number of repetitions of rebound sequences which act as indicators of a player's improvement.
The above sequences can be practiced using specific volleying techniques e.g. instep volley, the push (inside of the foot) volley, or the flick. The technique for the latter involves turning the ankle inwards as the player sets himself to contact the ball and then flicking the front outside of his foot at and through the ball at the last moment. Mastery of the volley flick allows a player to give every impression that he is about to bring the ball under control before flicking it away.

Progression 5.
Volleys alternate with half volleys.
A volley rebound is returned as a half volley ground pass against the angle of the wall and the ground. Given with top spin, the ground half volley 'kicks' upwards off the wall to ground angle' into the air and the volley sequence can be continued without any need to handle the ball.

Varying the target wall heights and the ground distances develops a player's 'feel' for the skills of soccer, the power which he needs to apply to the ball to achieve a certain result of height or distance or even of spin.

7.22 Controlling and Passing Sequences.
A volleying sequence is commenced using only the high wall mark. As the ball rebounds following the volley, the ball is controlled in the air using the technique for which practice is needed. The ball is made to drop to the ground close to the player and as 'softly' as possible. As it bounces it is volleyed or half volleyed back against the wall. The better the control, the less the bounce available for the return volley.

Two wall Practices.

Practicing between two walls, the player controls the ball in the air from the first wall while turning in the same movement. Having completed the turn, the player continues the sequence by volleying or half volleying the ball against the other wall and so on. Accuracy can be tested by drawing a circle about two feet in diameter on one wall. As a rebound is controlled in the air from on wall, the player turns and volleys or half volleys to hit the target circle with his second touch.

The various combinations of techniques possible in practice are limited only by a player's imagination when working against one or two walls.

Players must remember, however, that:
 a)   practice is most effective when a player sets himself something to achieve and practices until he can achieve his target consistently.
 b)   practice must be as realistic as possible. Even in singles practice, a player must imagine himself to be playing in a real game against live opponents.
 c)   practice should become progressively more difficult by limitation. . . bigger target scores, fewer touches, greater accuracy, smaller space, less time, smaller ball and so on.
 d)   skills and techniques practiced against a wall should be used (practiced) in a game situation as soon as possible. In practice matches, even in pick up, 'kick-about' games, a player should seek to use his new skills as much as possible. After all, if these games aren't for practice, what are they for?
 e)   Practice doesn't necessarily make perfect but the RIGHT sort of practice does.

The simpler the practice situation, e.g. one player by himself against a wall, the greater should be the player's demand on himself for perfection.

7.23 Back Heel Volleys.
Volley the ball against one wall, continuously or out of hand. As the ball rebounds off the wall and off the ground, the player turns away from it and flicks it with his heel overhead, or behind his back, onto the other wall. Skillful players can set up extended sequences using these techniques exclusively.

7.3 Doubles Practice.
Two players practicing together offer a much greater variety of practice possibilities, with a wall or without it. Their practice can be co-operative, where they help each other, or opposed, where they practice against each other.

7.31 Dribble To Score.
The practice area is about twenty yards by twenty yards. The goals, any sort of markers and two at each end, are five yards wide. The more skillful the players, the smaller the goals. Five yards in front of each goal and stretching across the whole

area at each end is a single line.

From his own end zone player A, using a soccer throw in technique, or any other soccer technique, throws to player B in his end zone. Player B controls the ball and tries to dribble past player A into A's end zone. B must challenge for possession out- side his end zone. A can score through either goal but only from within A's end zone.

If A challenges and gains possession of the ball he can counter attack into B's end zone but again he cannot score until he is inside that zone. Dribbling players who lose the ball have the immediate responsibility to get it back.

Attacking teams are most vulnerable to counter attack wherever and whenever they lose possession of the ball. A player's head drops in self commiseration; other players remonstrate with him and lose concentration while their opponents counter quickly to score: much quicker than it took me to write this.

Where the practice space is bounded on one side by a wall, the dribbling player can use the wall as his rebound surface giving him the option to dribble or to pass off the wall and dribble.

Dribbling games can take many forms according to which specific skills the players want to practice. For example, in the same area B, with the ball, faces his own end zone.

A takes up a position as close to him as he wishes. Clearly before B can dribble past his opponent he must turn with the ball. This is a situation in which mid-field players often find themselves in matches.

7.32 Wall Pass Or Dribble.

Playing alongside a wall or similar rebound surface, each player in turn tries to keep the ball for a set time (two minutes say) while making as many rebound passes against the wall as he can. He scores three points for every successful wall pass and one point if he dribbles successfully. If the practice is aimed principally at dribbling skills he scores three for dribbling success and one for a good wall pass.

Incentives and rewards are the motivating forces behind successful practice.

7.33 Control and Pass Contest.

(a) Player A volleys the ball out of his hands to player B, standing 10 or more yards away. B must control the ball and catch it in his hands before it touches the ground. As control improves, the players move further apart until the initial volleys are the equivalent, in the game, of high kicks.

Progressive difficulty and realism are created if the receiver, having controlled the ball within a required number of touches, returns the ball to the serving player who stands between two markers 8 yards apart. The players practice weak techniques or techniques using their weaker feet.

(b) As previously but having kicked towards B, player A must run out to make a challenge for the ball as soon as possible. The receiving player must make a first controlling touch while the ball is in the air before dribbling the ball to look for a scoring opportunity in the 'goal' behind player A.

7.4 Realistic Related Practice.

Sooner rather than later, techniques mastered after long hours of individual practice must be put to the test. The true test is in the player's ability to make his skill work against one or more opponents trying to stop him. Before this extreme test of ability is reached, most players need to move, successfully, through one or two additional stages.

To be effective, practice must finish with the player (or players) experiencing success. I never say never but practice must NEVER end with a poor performance or a failure.

Working with coaches at Turkey's leading club, Galatasaray of Istanbul, I watched international strikers practicing shooting skills. The practices were well organized, energetic and exceptionally disciplined. Additionally, they faithfully followed patterns of activity taken from the game, as all effective practices should. The professionalism of the whole set up was a credit to the international coaching courses in England where the coaches had been trained.

Shots came thick and fast for all of fifty minutes and the players applied themselves with commendable concentration. The trainers were astonished when I asked what the purpose of the practice had been. 'Goalscoring' was their obvious answer and they were dumbfounded when I asked them why, in that case, the players had been practicing missing!

Out of about one hundred shots at goal, perhaps forty hit the target, of which ten were saved or struck the goal posts and perhaps thirty scored. Sixty shots at goal missed the target altogether: some, it is true, by the narrowest of margins. The only conclusion possible from a seventy percent failure rate in relation to the practice aims was that the players had practiced missing!

Everyone enjoyed the session. . . and so did I. . . but they all agreed that practice was only valuable when it ended on a successful 'run' and when significantly more than fifty percent of the practice repetitions achieved the stated purpose of the practice. If 'shooting to hit the goal' had been the aim, the practice would still have failed; sixty percent missed. Shooting towards goal was all that was achieved and that was no sort of achievement for high class professionals.

The practice was easily adjusted by slowing the action down and insisting on higher degrees of accuracy. A player won three 'points' for any goal scored by hitting the inside of the side netting; two 'points' for any other goal scored and one point for each shot which the goalkeeper had to save. These incentives focused the concentration of the players on narrower objectives and thereby tested their control much more effectively.

'Tightening up' practice by rewarding different levels of attainment is important. Rewarding the high points scorers at the conclusion of practice, in front of all their team mates is another.

High class coaching is unrealizable unless the coach understands player motiva- tion. The clever use of incentive, rewards and especially recognition allows a coach to acknowledge individual player achievements and to adjust practice to meet individual players' needs.

The players' scores must be properly recorded so that each player knows what his success rate is and where he needs to improve. It is the coach's job. . . if he is a good one. . . to tell him and show him how.

7.41 Two v One Practice.

At the simplest level, there is no reason why a one to one practice shouldn't be opposed. Player A 'serves' the ball to player B who is practicing a particular technique. Having served the ball, A moves forward as quickly as he can to try to prevent. . . or to pretend to prevent. . . B from achieving his practice aim. The options open to B are now limited; more limited than they would be in the game perhaps. Nevertheless the threat of an opponent moving to interfere with his skill is a threat with which he must come to terms in the game itself.

All young players enjoy 'scrimmaging' in 1 v 1 or 2 v 1 situations. Hours and hours of scrimmaging on any spare piece of ground is how the world's greatest players became world class players.

(a) Dribbling and Shooting.

A suitable size goal is set up. A, the goalkeeper, can only move off his goal line when an opponent is about to shoot. B is an outfield defender and C is the attacker with the ball. C dribbles past B to shoot. Each player takes it in turn to play in each of the three positions.

Alternatively, B and C each try to score while opposing each other at the same time. Both are defenders when they haven't got the ball and either becomes the attacker when he has it. Now many more shots take place and the goalkeeper never knows from whom he is likely to receive the ball intentionally or otherwise.

Goalkeepers tell me that nowadays they are in greater danger from back passes than they are from opponents' shots!

Whenever the goalkeeper throws or kicks the ball into play there is immediately a struggle for possession which is exactly what mid-field players experience in the real game. As the players become more skillful, A 'doubles up' as goalkeeper and second out-field defender. This increases pressure on the single attacker but he is now able to score if he catches A far enough away from goal.

This is good practice for developing dribbling skill while rewarding the player who dribbles with his 'head up' looking for alternative options some distance away. Mid-field players need these skills and the 'vision' to go with them.

Where a practice grid is available, more specific skill practice is possible.

(b) 2 v 1, Dribbling and Passing.

Three players practice in a 30 yard x 20 yard area, zoned off into three 10 yard x 20 yard areas. Space per player is 200 square yards. Each player starts in a separate square. A throws or kicks the ball to B in his defensive 'half'. B uses a nominated skill to control the ball and/or pass it to player C. As soon as he has served the ball, A moves forward to oppose attempts by B and C to enter his defensive box at the end of which is a goal.

The attackers can only score from inside the 'goal area' but A must make at least one challenge for the ball before the opponents move it out of the mid-zone. If B is quick and accurate in controlling the first serve, he will be able to set up a dribbling or a dribbling and passing attack with C before A can gain a forward defending position.

(c) 1 v 2, Dribbling, Tackling and Shooting.

Here there are two small goals at A's end; each of the three players starts in a separate zone.

A and B are playing against C. A serves to C who controls and attacks B in the middle zone. Only B can defend in that zone. C must beat B before entering the scoring zone defended by A.

When C moves out of the middle zone, B can move back into A's end and become the goalline defender behind A. C can score through either of the two goals.

'Conditioned' Practice.

Practices can be adjusted to produce different effects. A player or players must play to a special rule or 'condition'. e.g. in the previous practice, 1 v 2, the receiver of the first serve might be 'conditioned' to make his first controlling touch before the ball bounces. This ensures that he practices aerial control. If there is a more precise need, the 'condition' might be that his first controlling touch must be with his chest (or with that surface for which he needs practice). If the receiver is a skillful dribbler who would benefit from stronger opposition, a suitable' condition' might require both A and B to be in the middle zone prepared to challenge as soon as C enters it.

7.42 Increasing Numbers.

Practice progression moves from 2 v 1 to 2 v 2, 3 v 2, 3 v 3, 4 v 3 and so on. Only where a player or players are exceptionally skillful will practice be numerically biased against him or them. e.g. 1 v 2, 2 v 3 and so on.

With very young players, it may be necessary to devise practices heavily biased towards a single player or towards the group who are intended as the main beneficiaries of the practice. Practices may be 4 v 2 or even 5 v 2 according to the degree of difficulty experienced by the players.

Practices must be adjusted to meet the capabilities of the players involved and allow for them to be reasonably successful, especially at the conclusion of practice. It is not necessary for players, to move through each stage when practicing. Stages are there for the convenience of players not to meet some preconceived process of teaching or coaching. For example, a top class player with a specific weakness may be placed by his coach into a most elementary 2 v 1 or 3 v 1 practice or even into an unopposed situation if there is a need for precise and careful development of a new technique or skill.

When describing practices here, the first number stated, e.g. the 3 in what is described as a 3 v 1 practice, represents the group which is the focus of the practice or which contains the player for whom the practice has been set up.

7.43 Even Practice. (e.g. 2 v 2, 4 v 4, 8 v 8)
Where there are even numbers in practice and two goals, the practice can be 'focused' by requiring all or certain players, to restrict their actions. e.g. 'No tackling' or 'Having received the ball, dribble past at least one opponent'. Failure to comply with a particular 'condition' results in ball possession being transferred to the other 'team'.

7.44 One Goal Practice.
In one goal, 'even' number practice, if the defending group needs a goalkeeper that group will have one outfield player fewer than their opponents. The extra player should give enough practice advantage to the attacking team and thereby enable the coach to direct the players' attentions towards specific practice objectives.

7.45 Two Goal Practice.
If a practice needs two goals, bias can be achieved by applying this condition:
  • whenever a team has the ball, all its players must become outfield attackers.
  • whenever a team hasn't the ball, one player must drop back onto the goal-line to become the goal defender. He alone can handle the ball.

The 'condition' affecting his position is important otherwise he can choose to be an out-field defender until it suits him to drop back into goal. This is likely to interfere with practice purpose.

7.44 'Odd' Practice.
Where practice involves an odd number, the group should be divided into two equal practice 'teams' with one player acting as a free player or 'floater'. If the practice has an attacking objective, the 'floater' joins whichever side has the ball; where the practice has a defensive purpose he joins the team which hasn't got the ball.

The 'floater' enables each team in turn to have the advantage of the extra player thus enabling that team to attack or defend as successfully as the practice objectives demand.

In attacking practice, both the floater and his 'new' team have to think quickly to exploit the extra player advantage. Similarly, the defending team which loses the floater's services whenever it give the ball away must adapt to the one player disadvantage even quicker!

The creation of extra player situations is a vital factor in setting up realistic, successful practice at all levels of the game.

7.5 Functional Practices.

Functional practices are devised to recreate the problems experienced by certain players, or groups of players, in particular phases of play; their problems will have been identified in match play.

Practices will be as closely related to match conditions as the paramount need for successful experience will allow. Although functional practices need to be as realistic as possible, they must be governed by the needs and the capabilities of the players upon whom practice is focused.

(a) Example: Playing Through Mid-field.

Practice Objectives.
Here, senior players are being coached to increase their perceptions of the need to:
- make space and time to give improved service to strikers.
- support the strikers to create more and better scoring opportunities.
- run the ball forward out of midfield and examine the need for interpassing alternatives.

In diagram 59 the three practice zones will be 20 yards deep by 70 or 60 yards wide. Midfield players are likely to find themselves playing a similar mid-field area during a game.

The higher the skill of the players the less the space.

The end zones are similar to the depth of the actual penalty area and they funnel into a final width of twenty yard, the width of an actual goal area.

Four midfield players are opposed by three. The four players play to create space and opportunities as specified in the practice objectives.

In each of the end zones is a goal, a goalkeeper and one striker opposed by one defender. The 'practice group' of midfield players play to create opportunities for one of their number to run the ball into the end zone. Their opponents work to prevent them doing so. A mid-field player's allowed to move into the end attacking zone only with the ball.

In the end zone he links up with the striker to exploit the 2 v 1 situation. The funneled end zone (made by using plastic ground markers or cones) means that the longer the attackers delay penetration, the easier it will be for the last defender on an

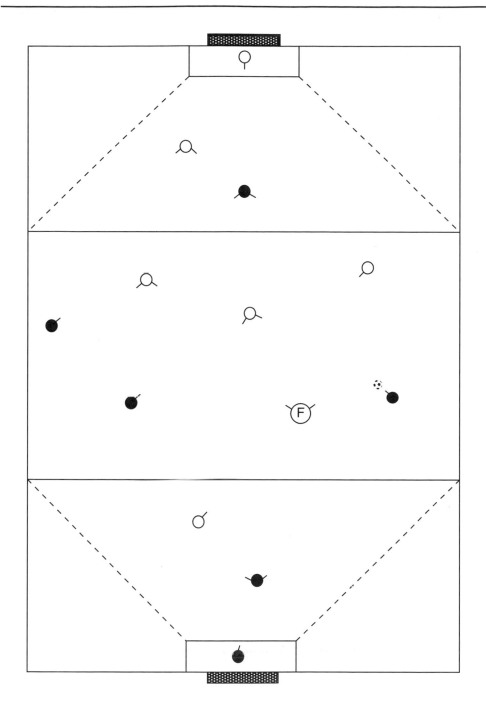

Diagram 59. Zonal practice for midfield attackers.

increasingly narrow front.

Similarly it will soon be apparent to defenders that if they can deflect their opponents into wide positions, penetration from those positions will be much more difficult. If the defending group of three gain possession they try to pass to the coach as accurately and as early as possible wherever he happens to be. The 'four group' must regroup very quickly to regain possession or prevent their opponents from finding the coach target.

Practice should always give an opposing group a chance of achieving something tangible. It keeps them interested and 'sharpens' the practice considerably.

This basic practice situation of 4 v 3 or 3 v 3. . . or however many midfield players the team deploys. . . can be adapted to expose any of the skills and tactical moves required of midfield players, in any phase of play.

With the addition of three more players, the practice can work in both directions, thereby intensifying it. A goalkeeper, a defender and a striker need to be deployed at the other end of the practice area. The 'odd' player needed in mid-field to set up 4 v 3 situations can play in both directions as the extra player.

Eventually the 4 v 3 will become 4 v 4 with the practice becoming almost fully realistic.

(b) A second example of functional practice for midfield players might be:
- to create effective, early pressure points at the front of the defending third of the pitch.
- controlling and deflecting opponents' attempts to penetrate this area.
- to exploit counter attacking chances from ball possession regained.

In diagram 60 there are three practice zones, each is 20 yards in depth and each is the full width of a normal pitch.

N.B. At the highest levels of play, coaches go to considerable lengths to know the actual pitch dimensions of all the clubs in their leagues so that their players can practice in realistic spaces according to whichever team they are playing next.

The black team's goalkeeper, with a 3:2 player advantage in his end zone, begins the attack. The player advantage increases the probability of a good service to the black midfield players in the middle zone. The four black players faced with four opponents try to play quality passes or run the ball, to the black strikers in the attacking end zone, for shots at goal.

Whenever the ball is moved into an end zone, the player giving the pass (or running the ball) can move forward to support the two strikers. When this occurs, one midfield defender can move into that end zone with him.

The objectives of the defending midfield players are:
- a) to prevent their opponents from turning when receiving the ball.
- b) to put any opponent under severe pressure should he receive the ball and turn to face the goal towards which his team is attacking.

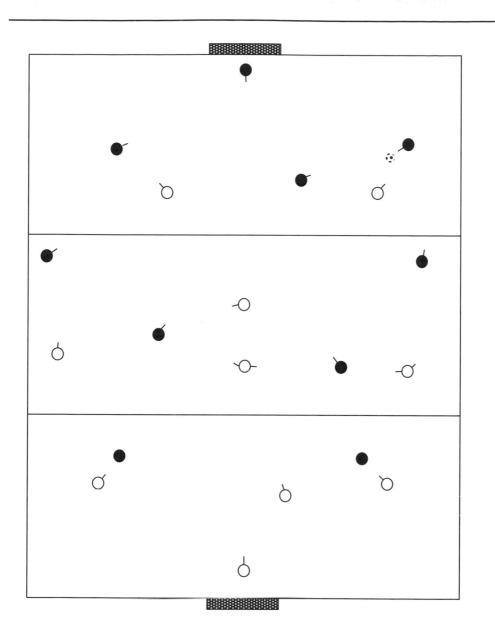

Diagram 60. Attack and counter attack in mid-field.

c) to compel the opposing mid-field players to choose 'square' or 'back' passes rather than forward passes, thereby increasing the probability of interceptions.

d) having regained possession, mid-field players furthest from the ball immediately take up blindside positions preparatory to moving forward.

Except as stated above, initially all the players are restricted to the zones in which they commence the practice.

A progression from the above would be to reduce the number of defending midfield players to three. Initially, the width of the midfield zone would be reduced at the same time but later expanded to the normal pitch width.

This practice is excellent for coaching defending midfield players in 'splitting' and 'jockeying' opponents, especially where the attack has an extra player. All attacking play aims at creating situations in which an attacking team has an extra player near to the ball. . . or it should! The practice is also effective for developing agility and speed in adjusting defensive positions across a wide front.

The extension of the practice into the respective end zones adds the degree of realism and 'release' necessary if players are to commit themselves wholeheartedly to improvement through practice.

Functional practices are easy to devise if players (or coaches) can 'call up' match situations out of their experience and reconstruct the essential elements in a small game form. Above all, it is absolutely vital that the total area in which practice takes place is a replica of the actual action area in the game itself.

Chapter 8
Training

Broadly speaking, the younger the player the more he (or she) should concentrate on scrimmaging practice in small game situations. . . 1 v 1, 2 v 2, 3 v 3, and so on. Very young players, five, six and seven years of age committing most of their playing time to games of this kind will become skillful soccer players. They will acquire the techniques of the game because they will have to.

Exposure to game play, even in its crudest form, continually poses new problems for young players; they learn best by imitating better players, by trying things for themselves, often by themselves.

Solutions to problems 'discovered' by players themselves are infinitely better than learning by instruction. Of course clever teachers often provide the direction in which answers are most likely to be found without players realizing it.

This acquisition of skill through massive exposure to play occupies many hours a day. Consequently the young player's physical commitment is enormous. The only fitness extra to ball play should be running. Success in soccer comes that much less readily for people who have poor athletic capacities. In soccer these are the ability to sprint very quickly over relatively short distances and the capacity for sustaining medium paced running interspersed with short sprints while exercising the skills of the game.

From five years of age children should run, in one way or another, for at least two miles each day but not all at once. From seven or eight years until ten or eleven, the distance should be two to three miles. From early adolescence the distance might be increased to between three and four miles. This is not to say that they should complete these distances in one continuous run but during the course of the day they should run, at mixed pace, distances from a quarter mile up to half a mile, making up the target distances recommended. And this, as I have already said, should be in addition to soccer scrimmaging and other soccer related play or practice. What is absolutely certain is that the foundations for leg strength, speed and the general endurance needed to carry a player through the game are better laid early rather than late.

The only other characteristic which merits attention at very early ages is that of suppleness, the ability to move all of the major joint-complexes as far as necessary to allow all the movements of the game to be executed without stress or strain. This really is a matter for physical education teachers in school but in the lower reaches of school life, many teachers lack the experience to recognize unnecessary joint stiffness and the expertise to do something about it. Once again, the sooner a diagnosis is made, the easier it is to do something about it. Very young children should be very supple in all the major joint complexes. If they aren't it might be as well to consult an orthopedic specialist. Later in this chapter you will find suppling exercises and activities which in themselves act as rough diagnostic tests of this quality.

Specific, directed athletic and gymnastic training should not be necessary before eleven years of age other than where serious physical deficiencies are noted in young players. When that occurs, parents, teachers and coaches should seek expert advice if they do not possess expertise themselves. . . and they should watch out for well-meaning amateurs or self anointed experts; they are dangerous!

The principles and details of progressive planned practice and training for players at all stages of development are beyond the scope of this book but the following generalized ideas and recommendations have stood the test of my own experience and knowledge.

The practice and training of soccer players should be developed around the five S's: Skill, Speed, Strength, Stamina and Suppleness.

The younger the player the greater the proportion of time devoted to technical quality and cleverness. Group interaction occurs voluntarily around ten years of age: earlier for those from soccer environments and later for those whose backgrounds are less soccer orientated.

In professional and senior soccer generally, where team results assume greater importance, team and group skill will be given higher priorities in the allocation of preparation time but both depend upon technical effectiveness of course. Nevertheless the older the player, above the mid twenties say, the less the return he is likely to achieve from time devoted to trying to learn new techniques. Maintaining and raising the quality of the player's existing techniques is another matter and well worth the time given to it. The older the player the less likely he is to increase the range of his technical skills but there are players who have extended the range of their techniques to quite advanced ages.

Their secret, probably, is in their sheer love of technical expression. Similarly with fitness, the older the player the greater the need for gaining and maintaining appropriate levels of fitness. It must be reiterated that much of the technical and tactical work can contain significant fitness elements.

The following matrix, diagram 61 may be a useful basis upon which levels of training and practice may be developed. The matrix is a guide and its use a matter of judgment and of opinion.

Within the general consideration of fitness, the proportions of time allocated to speed, strength, stamina and suppleness should be based upon an individual player assessment. All things being equal, I would give more time to speed (and agility) than to the others. Speed and agility work can be adapted easily to include stamina and strength elements. Similarly stamina would be given more consideration than strength and suppleness.

Training bias would be determined by individual player needs and by the development stages through which all young people pass.

Practice and training priorities must meet specific player needs which may change from time to time to meet special conditions and different seasonal demands, especially in countries where major changes in climatic conditions occur.

	3-6	7-10	11-13	14-16	17-19	Senior
			YEARS			
Team Skill	-	-	10	15	20	25
Group Skill	-	20	20	25	25	25
Technique	90	70	55	45	35	30
Fitness	10	10	15	15	20	20

Diagram 61. Percentage of total practice time allocated to different aspects of player development according to age.

Certain players may require special training or practice from time to time which will necessitate one of the 'S's moving above others in priority. Nevertheless, the more permanent the change in the order, the more likely it is that coaches have got their priorities wrong or haven't established any priorities at all!

If teams decide to forsake skill for effort and intimidation, the 'S' formation can be in any sort of order. . . confusion might be a better word.

This happened in England where many professional teams decided that players trained to play like fast moving 10,000 metre runners stood every chance of overwhelming more skillful but less athletic opponents; they failed spectacularly. The result was that English teams had large numbers of powerful medium paced runners, most of whom lost whatever individual skill they ever had. Predictably, the effects upon the quality of play in the top English leagues and consequently in the national team have been catastrophic.

It is relatively easy to persuade skillful players to work harder from time to time; it is very difficult to cause hard running players to improve the range and quality of their skills. Skill is infinitely harder to acquire than athletic condition; it is also infinitely easier to lose.

Training Activities.
Agility Speed.
In diagram 62 a small starting and finishing circle is central to four 'flagged stations'. The distance between the centre circle and each flag is ten yards. Player P starts and finishes inside the centre circle. He completes the four legs working clockwise.

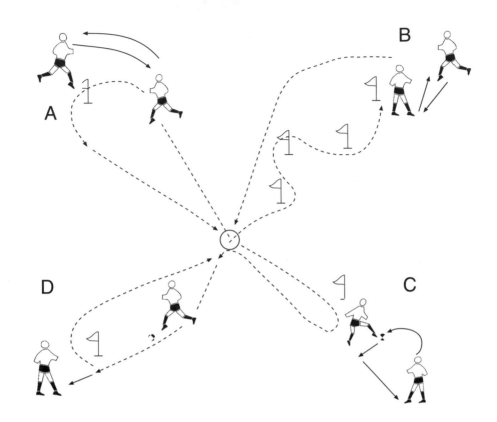

Diagram 62. Agility, Speed training.

At each station, marked by a flag or post, a serving player waits with a ball. Starting from the circle, P runs towards station A where, before he reaches the flag the ball is served to him in the air. P must jump off the ground to head the ball back to A. Having completed the header, P continues his run around the flag and back to touch the inside of the centre circle with his hand.

Now P moves to station B, zig-zagging in and out of the marker cones as he does so. Beyond the flag at B, P receives and returns a pass from the server and runs directly back to touch down in the centre circle.

Next he moves towards station C where, having passed the flag, he controls the ball served to him in the air, brings it down and passes it back to the server. He must touch the ball at least twice before returning to touch down inside the starting circle.

Finally, he moves to station D. Half way towards the flag he receives a ground pass and returns it after passing the flag. He runs round the flag and returns to touch down in the centre circle.

The four station run is completed as quickly as possible and the player's time recorded. The training objective is to improve speed within the context of soccer agility. Skill accuracy and control are of minor importance in this activity.

The five players rotate to fulfill each function, including the high speed run.

In one training session each of the five players should complete five runs, depending upon their starting levels of capability. They will work up to seven such runs over a period of several weeks.

Obstacle Runs.

A simple obstacle course can be used for a similar training effect.

In diagram 63 the length of the run is twenty five yards each way. The obstacles are designed to break up players' running patterns. If there is a squad of players in training. . . let's say eighteen. . . three obstacle runs can be set out and the training can be conducted competitively on a relay basis, six players to a team. Each player in a team must complete a 'set' of five runs, i.e. the team of six completes 30 runs.

The first team to finish wins. One player runs while five wait their turn and recover. A 'set' of five repetitions with five rest intervals should enable each player to give maximum effort for each run. As the players gain fitness over a period of six to eight weeks say, the race is repeated two, three, four and up to a maximum of five times in a single training session. In other words the players are sprinting for five sets of five repetitions (runs) per set. Between each set or if you like between each race, the players must be allowed to recover. The highest possible level of performance is the training aim.

Increasing the Loading.

To increase the training 'load', the runs can be carried out on sloping ground. The starting circle is lower down the slope than each of the four stations which fan out above it. The distance between the lower station and the stations above it is 15 yards.

Alternatively, these shuttle runs as they are known may take place on flat soft ground, even on sand. Low resistant ground conditions make sprinting that much harder and the training that much more effective. Muscular contraction has to be that much more powerful to achieve the same thrust as from firm ground. Agility speed training carried out in soft sand makes the work extremely demanding.

Where training is carried out in unusual ground conditions, it is important. . . as always. . . that players have completed a thorough warm-up and stretching routine before taking on these exacting runs. It is also important that they wear the right sort of footwear.

Stamina and Strength.

Stamina (Endurance) is the capacity of a player to resist the onset of tiredness and fatigue, for ninety minutes in the case of senior players, to enable him to use his skills as accurately and as perceptively as possible to achieve optimum effect. Stamina training aims to strengthen (increase the power of) the heart and the lungs when

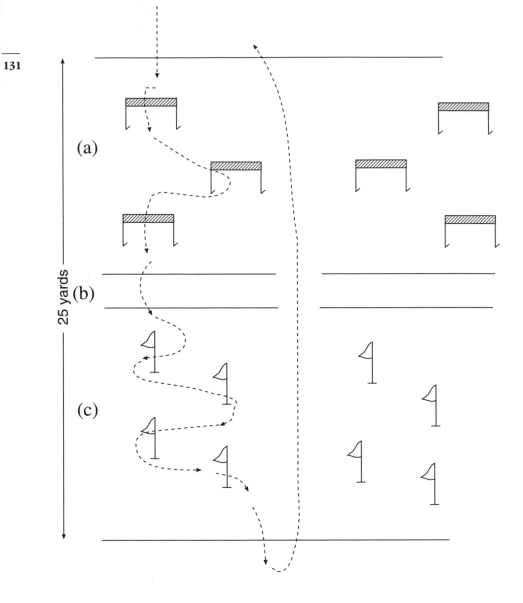

25 yards

(a)

(b)

(c)

Diagram 63. Obstacle Course
     at (a) hurdles: 'over, under, over'
     at (b) 'stream' 12 ft wide
     at (c) weave run.

taking in air and when using oxygen to fuel exercise.

Air (Oxygen), taken in by the lungs as a result of increasing the rate of breathing, is pumped by the heart into circulation more efficiently, i.e. with fewer heart beats per minute, to those parts of the body which are working hard and which demand increased fuel. Without oxygen, parts of the body or all of it will gradually stop working.

Stamina training enables the working parts of the body to become more efficient in the use (the taking up) of oxygen and also in the exchange process by which the waste products of exercise are expelled through the lungs. Waste products must be cleared from the body before its parts can be re-fueled for further action.

We can consider stamina needs in two parts. The first is general stamina which is based upon increasing the efficiency of the heart: lung relationship. The second is the heart: muscle relationship which enables particular groups of muscles to go on working reasonably efficiently for long periods while enduring difficult conditions e.g. extreme climatic conditions or when called upon to contract repeatedly without being permitted to relax and recover.

The first, general stamina, is also known cardio-respiratory (CR) endurance; the second, cardio-vascular (CV) endurance. The two are closely inter-dependent.

Improvement in CR Stamina (Endurance).

1. Steady state (continuous) training.
A period of moderately intense activity, although not necessarily the same activity, lasting for not more than thirty minutes. The activity is continuous and sustained without rest.

The training activity can be:

a) even paced running over a fixed course (distance) e.g. round a track.

b) repeated runs around a fixed course which includes fixed obstacles and different gradients.

c) running around a course to repeat certain soccer skills at certain points during each circuit.

In a - c, see diagram 63, players may be required to cover a fixed number of laps of the course in the shortest possible time (the time not to exceed 30 minutes). Alternatively, players may be required to run for a fixed period of time (up to 30 minutes) while trying to complete as many circuits as possible of the courses described in 1 to 3 previously.

d) soccer play in such a form as to guarantee sustained periods of fairly hard to hard running. e.g.

Whichever form the stamina training takes, the player spreads his effort evenly over the whole period trying to complete the training task as efficiently as he can.

Progressive loading is achieved when the player:

    a) reduces his time for a given distance or

    b) covers an increased distance in the same time or

    c) increases the distance AND reduces his time.

Steady state training is useful for establishing and maintaining a basic level of general stamina (endurance).

Interval training.

This training involves a number of intervals of hard running; each interval of hard work is followed by a suitable interval of less intensive activity which permits the player to partially recover from the preceding interval of hard work,

Interval training improves players' tolerance of random, repeated high levels of stress on the heart and on the muscles. The total time allocation for interval training can be based on the known distances covered during a game by senior players. The total distance covered during a match, by the hardest working players (mid-field players) has been found to be as much as 6,000 yards and that by mid-field players. Of those 6,000 yards, about 2,500 yards were covered at speed and the single sprints varied between 10 yards and 50 yards. In soccer related interval training therefore, it would seem that a player should train to cover a total of 2,500 yards in intensive but sub-maximal intervals of about 40 yards. That means about 60 repetitions of the intensive intervals. Partial recovery must be allowed between each intensive interval. For players at moderate levels of fitness this will be up to five times the time taken during the work interval. As players become fitter, the recovery interval will be reduced progressively until the recovery interval is twice the duration as the work interval.

Both steady state and interval training develop the player's capacity to work under stress but never without being able to take in and use oxygen. In other words, they are both aerobic training methods.

Soccer players are never exposed to levels of stress which require them to continue playing while being unable to take in oxygen. Anaerobic training is not necessary for soccer players. If both are incorporated in the same training session, steady state work should be completed first.

The recovery periods should be active. A player should continue jogging around until his next work interval. Where a number of soccer players are training together, they should practice a soccer skill or skills in pairs.

Without affecting the level of intensity during the work interval, soccer activities or movements should feature prominently in the training run.

Power (Strength) Training.

A soccer player needs power to give him a winning start whenever he has to sprint to get to the ball first: to make an interception or a tackle. Soccer players, unlike track sprinters, must start powerfully from any manner of starting positions. They may be moving away from the direction towards which, eventually, the sprint must be made. They may be falling or actually on the ground when they are required to move as fast as possible to join the action in another part of the field. To get up, into a sprinting stride, and hit top speed within four or five yards demands considerable leg power.

Mid-field players are often involved in man to man contests for the ball or for positions in which they can receive or tackle for it. Modern soccer demands that of all the players, the mid-field player must have power. Other players may have rest periods when the action moves away. Mid-field players are the perpetual motion men and they have to have the 'engine' and the power to carry them through.

Perhaps the best example of mid-field power in recent times has been Diego Maradonna, the Argentinian pocket Hercules, who drove Napoli in Italy from nowhere to a leading position in world club soccer. From his first appearance as a world class player ten years ago, Maradonna seemed to be built of muscle: muscle which exploded him into action with or without the ball at his feet: muscle which gave him gravity defying balance when the laws of physical science said that he must fall: muscle which he could call on to hit a pass effortlessly, radar accurately, to a team mate stealing behind defenders sixty yards away.

Soccer playing power is a player's capacity for using the strength, in any relevant muscle group, at speed to exert force against a resistance of some kind. Strength is a person's capacity to cause any relevant muscle group to contract effectively against resistance of some kind: usually that means to move it. Pure athletic or 'movement' strength is not a problem for soccer players since the resistances they are concerned with moving. . . the ball, their own bodies, occasionally the body of another player, when charging or being charged. . . are usually well within their strength capacities.

If a player has to tackle a much heavier and more powerful opponent, inclined to violence, Wade's law should be applied. It states that,

"It's better to be a coward on the field, than a hero in hospital."

Increased power will be required when the game is played under exceptionally heavy ground conditions, in snow or in similarly exacting weather conditions.

"Power (strength applied at speed) for a soccer player is best achieved by:
   • practicing and playing on a quite steeply sloping area end to end.
   • practicing and playing on a very soft surface e.g. dry sand, heavy mud or thick grass.
A soft or cloying training surface requires players to increase the speed and quality of muscular contraction when running or jumping.
      • practicing while wearing heavy boots and/or while wearing a jacket incorporating pockets with weights inside.
      • running against the resistance of someone or something pushing or pulling back against the direction of thrust.

All work carried out against appropriate resistance will improve power: weight training certainly will. Speaking personally I would prefer to adapt soccer skill practices wherever possible. The transfer of training effects, I think, is best achieved within the context of soccer situations.

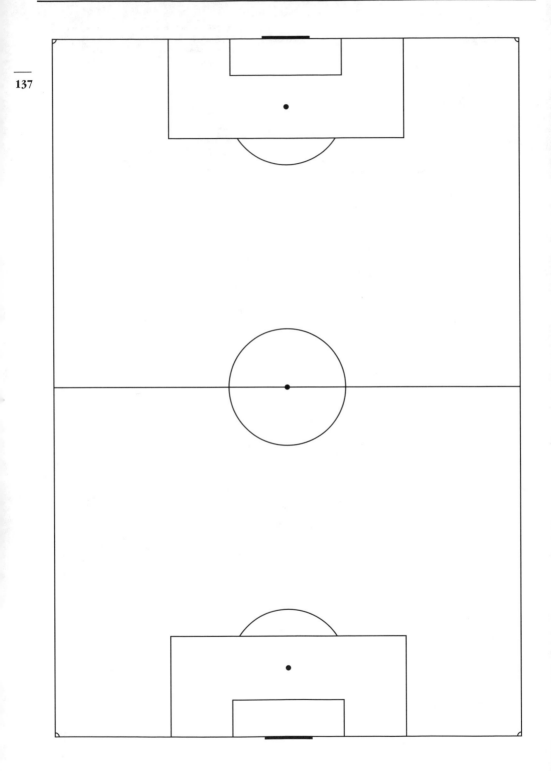

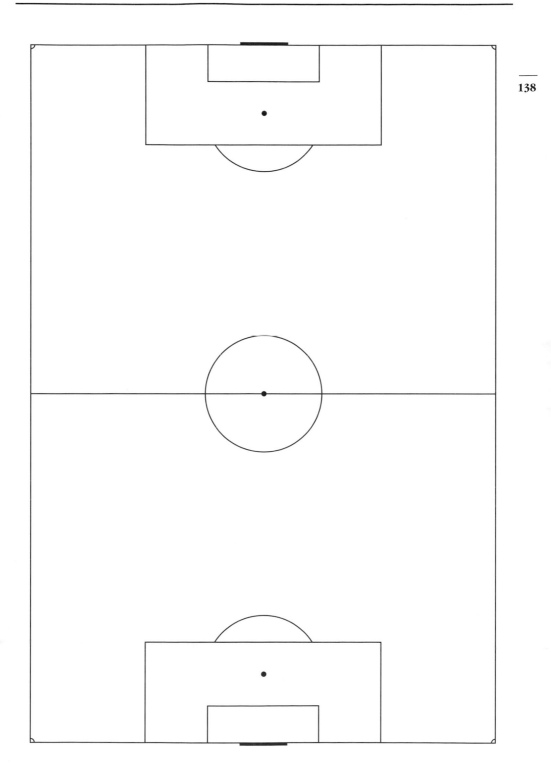

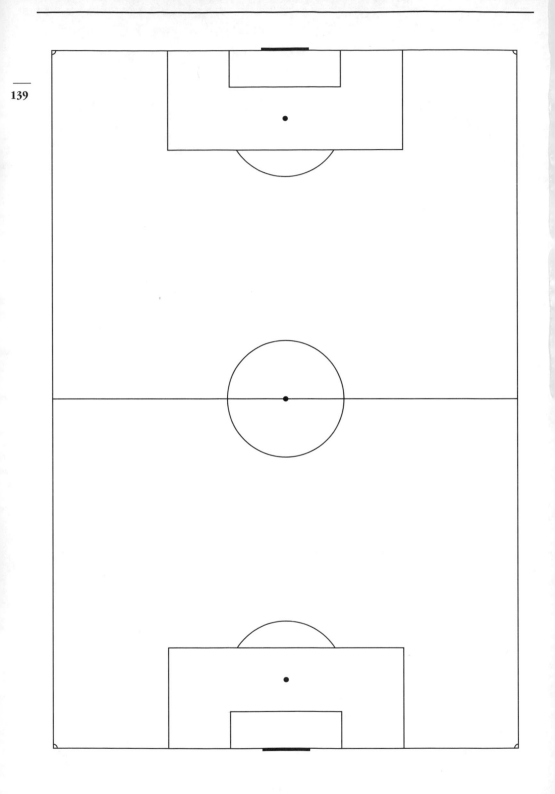

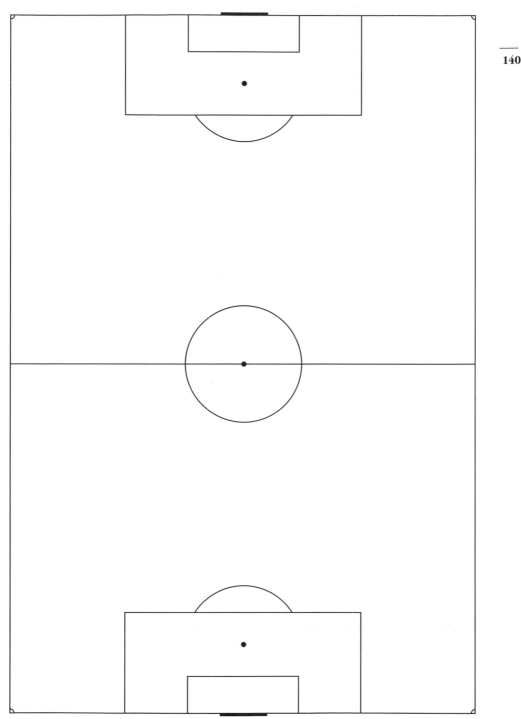

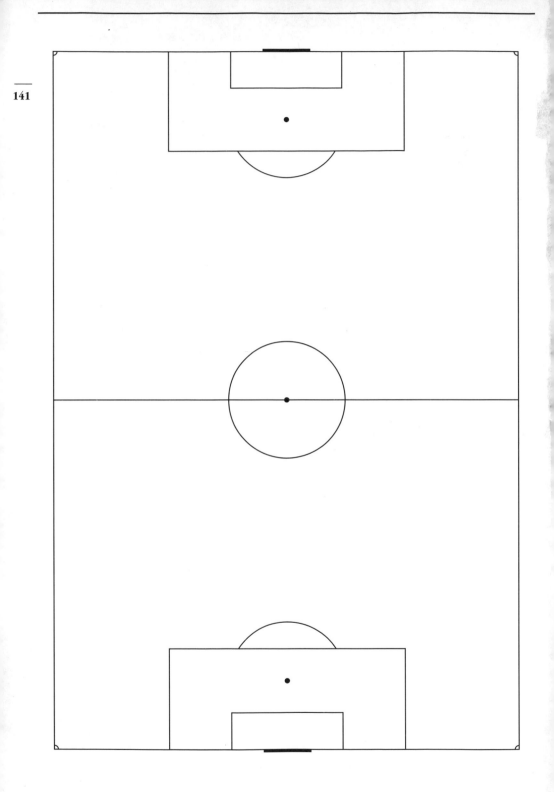